Hope Rising by Jacob Isaac is an inspiring book written to encourage readers that God cares for his people perhaps the most when life seems darkest. The author reminds us that many things in our lives can be discouraging or even detrimental. Hard times will come, but that's not the end of the story. First, we must accept difficulties, and then we begin to try and understand them, not only the toll they take on us, but what we can learn – patience, humility and trust in the One who can help. From there, the book offers a meaningful range of tools that enable us to make sense out of suffering and loss. Mr Isaac's optimism points the way to comfort, peace, and restoration through faith. Everyone can benefit from the message of this book.

D. L. Christian, PhD
Author & Editor

This book is a must-read for everyone in the Body of Christ in search of biblical hope.

Henry Abraham, CADC
Founder, CEO, Sobriety Society International
www.sobrietysocietyintl.com

So much happens every day. We may change ourselves for the better; our lives may open more than we ever imagined. How do we manage such transformations? Our complex, yet personal human lives may reveal many wonders, obstacles and ways forward. What do we need to guide us?

Books such as *Hope Rising* assisted me to develop an adult life with much success. I believe teenagers through to adults could also learn excellent techniques for changing mindsets, understanding the fullness of faith and how to enter into trustworthy, beneficial relationships. I recommend this carefully written volume, offering fine assistance, readily tailored to suit many individuals who seek better.

Raewyn Alexander BIC
Author, Editor & Publisher

HOPE
RISING

HOPE RISING

FINDING HOPE WHEN
YOU'RE FEELING LOST

JACOB ISAAC

Hope Rising
Published by Jacob Isaac
New Zealand

© 2020 Jacob Isaac

ISBN 978-0-473-51469-3 (Softcover)
ISBN 978-0-473-51470-9 (ePUB)
ISBN 978-0-473-51471-6 (Kindle)

Editing:
Keitha Smith, Debra Johanyak & Andrew Killick

Production & Typesetting:
Lizelle Windon & Andrew Killick
Castle Publishing Services
www.castlepublishing.co.nz

Cover design:
Paul Smith

Scriptures taken from the Holy Bible,
New International Version®, NIV®.
Copyright © 1973, 1978, 1984, 2011 by Biblica, Inc.™
Used by permission of Zondervan.
All rights reserved worldwide.

ALL RIGHTS RESERVED

No part of this publication may be reproduced, stored in a retrieval system, or transmitted in any form or by any means, electronic, mechanical, photocopied or recorded, or otherwise, without the prior permission of the copyright owner, except for brief quotations included in a review of the book.

The stories shared by others in this publication are based on real life events. The names of those involved have been changed to protect their privacy.

First and foremost, to my Lord Jesus Christ – my Saviour, Sanctifier and friend – whose love, grace and mercy continually astounds me: I dedicate this book to your honour and glory.

To my gorgeous and charming daughter, Christine Jade Isaac, for your love, patience and encouragement. You had to endure so much when I was in the ministry, and have so gracefully handled all the challenges that have occurred in our lives.

I am immensely proud of you and will always love you.

Also to the people that have been pivotal in shaping my life. I want to honour my spiritual mum and dad, Dr Joseph and Dolores D'Allende, for your unconditional love, prayers and support over the years; for imparting and depositing in me the spiritual wealth of God's Word; for believing in me and seeing what I couldn't – my God-given potential and calling. You have inspired me and given me hope beyond measure, which is now evident in the publishing of this book; your labour has not gone in vain. From the depths of my heart I love you and thank you. 'Therefore, brethren, stand fast and hold the traditions which you were taught, whether by word or our epistle.' (2 Thessalonians 2:15)

Foreword

Life isn't always easy. We all know that. But sometimes it isn't even *enjoyable or bearable*, depending on our circumstances at the time. While we long for days that spill into weeks and months of easy living, total fulfilment, and a deep sense of belonging and purpose, the truth is that while these long stretches of good times certainly do exist, they're sometimes bookended with trials and tribulations that take the wind right out of our sails.

When the crashing waves do come, we often find ourselves feeling down, frustrated, and angry. We might feel alone, even when surrounded by family and friends. And if we're a believer, now's as good a time as any for the doubts to creep in.

Why did God allow this pain?
Can He hear my prayers?
Does He even care?
Where is He anyway?

Jacob Isaac is no stranger to the world's injustices. As a young man, he quickly learned that the world isn't always a safe place, even in one's own community. Growing up in poverty, abused and mistreated during the brutal years of South African apartheid, Jacob's self-esteem, confidence, and drive dwindled away. It seemed he would never achieve his dreams. Until one day, he dared to hope in something greater than himself.

As he sought guidance from mentors and began to focus on the goodness in life, instead of the often-overwhelming dark clouds of circumstance, he developed new ways of thinking. His outlook on life renewed day by day, and he began to see that hope could strengthen almost anyone's heart and mind, even after unimaginable ordeals.

He writes this book on hope, sharing his discoveries to inspire others, so that they may find strength within. He has experienced the deepest despair. And he's also come out of it stronger, happier, and excited to share this same hope and enthusiasm with others.

Even when it feels as though all hope is lost, we only have to look back at how far we've come to see that there was always a way through, even when we did not believe it was possible. With each sunrise, hope can illuminate even the darkest corners of life, if we allow it to.

By focusing on the insightful stories within this book, along with sound biblical references and examples, Jacob shows how you can change your thinking, even if you can't immediately change your circumstances. With persistence and a desire for change, you can move from hopelessness to *hopeful*, use your bad experiences for good, and plan for a more positive future.

A greater understanding of God's love is just up ahead.

Hope Rising can help you assess your life, rediscover lost dreams, and find a better and closer relationship with God. Take the first step on a journey to a more hopeful you today.

Alice Sullivan, Writer and Editor
www.alicesullivan.com

Contents

Foreword — 9
Introduction — 15

1. Purpose and Perspective — 17
2. Mindset Matters — 31
3. Entitlement and Expectation — 47
4. Updating Your Understanding — 65
5. Mighty is our Master — 77
6. Significant Suffering — 91
7. Glorious Gratitude — 109
8. Re-examining and Reframing — 125
9. An Outward Focus — 141
10. Now and Next — 151

Final Thoughts — 161
Help Directory — 163
Acknowledgements — 165
About the Author — 167

INTRODUCTION

Let's be honest. If this book has made it into your hands, chances are you're feeling a little short on hope right now. If so, welcome. You've come to the right place. I think I can help.

I cannot know your unique life circumstances – what events or insults or rejections or grief have made you begin to lose hope. Life is certainly not easy for some of us. Over the coming chapters we will explore many aspects of life – both internal and external – and look at how you might be able to regain what you've lost. Make no mistake; hope is a vital part of the human experience. It's as important as breathing. Without hope, many lost souls will wither and die.

At the outset, I'd like you to know that I've had my fair share of difficulties. I know what it's like to see plans collapse, to stop believing I'll finish a demanding task, to feel like I've forgotten my dreams. Some life experiences have hurt my body, bent my mind, twisted my thoughts, and made me give up. Disturbing events changed my life's direction, shocked me, and caused me to view daily life as unpleasant, with all that I loved seemingly damaged. I have experienced poverty, abuse, apartheid, divorce, and other painful struggles and losses. I know what it's like to lose hope, but I also know what it's like to find it again – to see light break through the bleakness.

When you lose something you hold very dear – a family member, a friend, a loved one, your sense of home – the consequences may be staggering. You can lose your balance mentally, emotionally, and spiritually. You might feel so broken and alone that normalcy may seem permanently out of reach. Many people experience those losses and express hopelessness as a result. But God is good – always. He loves you and me – always. He has answers – always. We just have to develop the habit of turning to Him and seeking His wisdom and comfort to survive and eventually even thrive.

This book offers solace and guidance to those who have lost hope or who are finding hope difficult to grasp or maintain. This information is not intended to be a substitute for medical or professional advice. If you are suffering from clinical depression, are thinking of harming yourself, are in a situation involving abuse, or find yourself in dire circumstances beyond your control, I encourage you to seek professional help. There are wonderful people who care and are able to walk through that situation with you. Make every effort to find those compassionate experts who can provide professional assistance for serious issues.

It is common for most people to go through a valley of darkness at some point in their lives – maybe more than once. Let's explore the challenges of despair together and be as authentic as possible. Let's reflect on the past, examine the present, and look to the future with honesty. Hope is a thing of beauty and is best examined in the light of faith.

CHAPTER ONE

Purpose and Perspective

Life can be cruel. People are often hurtful. Relationships fail, or a loved one leaves. Sometimes our journey takes us on a direct path to connecting with our goals and dreams. Other times, that journey detours to the not-so-scenic route of delay or even failure. At times, the pursuit of goals and dreams can seem like an impossibility. It is too hard. There isn't enough time. Money and resources are scarce. No one wants to help. You feel like giving up because your once-dynamic dreams have crumbled.

But lost hope can be regained. Life goes on, day by day – there are ups and downs. What is true for you right now might be difficult, or even overwhelming, but circumstances don't necessarily have to stay that way. Whatever you are going through, or whatever crisis might be looming on the horizon, a thorough understanding of hope – of what it is, where it comes from, and what influences it – will help you put the situation into much-needed perspective for clarity and renewal

What is hope?

The *Oxford Dictionary* defines hope as follows:

1. expectation and desire, e.g. for a certain event to occur; and
2. a person, thing, or circumstance that encourages hope. It's a word we often use lightly: 'I hope to see you later'; 'I hope it's chicken for dinner'; 'I hope I don't miss the bus.' It's also used in more important situations: 'I hope I get into university'; 'I hope it's not cancer'; 'I hope we make it out of this alive.'

Hope's various meanings can undermine and muddy the seriousness of this characteristic. But, ultimately, they all have one thing in common – they look to a future event with the desire to see a positive outcome. Hope, then, keeps us looking forward with optimism. While the use of the word can be trivial, its importance shouldn't be underestimated. It's so important, in fact, that the Bible lists it as a key virtue for life.

You may be familiar with 1 Corinthians 13, a much-quoted chapter about love. At the end of the chapter comes verse 13:

And now these three remain: faith, hope and love. But the greatest of these is love.

The inclusion of hope here is interesting. We all know that love is critical. We need it, we crave it, and it makes us feel secure. We give love and receive it. The Bible famously states that

God so loved the world that he gave his one and only Son... (John 3:16)

When you consider these words, can there be a more meaningful expression of love than someone dying to save your life?

Faith is also vital. Without it, we would have no relationship with God. The Book of Hebrews defines faith this way:

> ...being sure of what we hope for and certain of what we do not see. (Hebrews 11:1)

In the same chapter we are told that

> without faith it is impossible to please God, because anyone who comes to him must believe that he exists and that he rewards those who earnestly seek him. (Hebrews 11:6)

So, why is hope included with two such vital facets of our lives? Could it be because hope allows us to continue to love and believe despite difficult circumstances? Could it be that, without hope, we would experience difficulty in expecting the best of people, maintaining feelings of optimism, or trusting God?

The three core virtues of faith, hope, and love share interesting commonalities that invite comparison and analysis.

FAITH, HOPE, AND LOVE ALL DISPLAY AN EXTERNAL COMPONENT

External love is, without a doubt, the easiest to understand. God's love is external, coming to us in the earthly sphere from His heavenly realm. If we are fortunate, our parents' love for each other and us as their children has provided a firm foundation of stability for our lives. We also may have received the love of friends or have experienced romantic love. This type of love plays a major role in who we are and what we think about ourselves because we often consciously or unconsciously seek validation and affection as confirming our worth. While we may have a personal, internal sense of who we are and our value to this world, experiencing support and encouragement from others reinforces our foundational beliefs about ourselves.

Faith, too, can come from external sources. If people display great faith in themselves – or place their faith in us – it can inspire us to live up to the trust extended to us. Similarly, people can offer hope, and such hope, newly discovered or rekindled, can make all the difference in tough times. Sometimes, all it takes is a small word of encouragement to lift our spirits, to make us feel that everything will be okay. You can probably recall an uplifting card in the mail, a text message on your phone, a computer email, or a heart-warming phone call that reawakened your faith in human nature and reignited your hope in God's providence. Kind words spoken in a time of need are like medicine to a broken spirit:

> A word fitly spoken is like apples of gold in pictures of silver. (Proverbs 25:11 KJV)

FAITH, HOPE, AND LOVE ALL HAVE AN INTERNAL COMPONENT

Although feelings should not be relied upon entirely as an accurate indication of what is true, faith, hope, and love can be experienced internally as emotions. They are influenced by what goes on in our hearts and minds, and are, to some extent, governed by thoughts, attitudes, experiences, and opinions. We can talk ourselves into almost anything – good or bad. To complicate things, Satan creeps near, whispering words of condemnation and hopelessness in our ears. Our self-esteem may be so fragile that a critical but well-intended word from a friend, relative, or co-worker can send us spiralling into a sea of anguish. As William Shakespeare's Hamlet pointed out in his eponymous play, 'for there is nothing either good or bad, but thinking makes it so' (*Hamlet* II:2).

God advises us in the Bible through the Apostle Paul:

> Finally, brethren, whatever is true, whatever is honourable, whatever is right, whatever is pure, whatever is lovely, whatever is of good repute, if there is any excellence and if anything worthy of praise, dwell on these things. (Philippians 4:8)

The Bible points out that we can control our thoughts, and we ought to focus on positive mental ideas and images that bring us close to God.

FAITH, HOPE, AND LOVE ALL REQUIRE AN ELEMENT OF ACTION

1 Corinthians 13 defines love in verses 4 to 7:

> Love is patient, love is kind. It does not envy, it does not boast, it is not proud. It is not rude, it is not self-seeking, it is not easily angered, it keeps no record of wrongs. Love does not delight in evil but rejoices with

the truth. It always protects, always trusts, always hopes, always perseveres.

Many of these facets of love require us to take specific action. For example, have you ever become impatient with a child who is not focusing on household chores or homework? Have you ever been mean-spirited to a family member or friend? Do you feel jealous of the neighbour's new car? Do you lose your temper easily when tired or ill? Do you envy the success of others – or secretly hope they will fail? Attitudes like these chisel away at potential love for others in our hearts. Jesus taught us that we are to care about other people as much as we care for ourselves, or perhaps even more. In loving others, we reflect God's love for us. Love of all types inspires hope in the giver and receiver.

In Mark 12:33, Jesus explains how God wants us to love:

> And to love him with all the heart, and with all the understanding, and with all the soul, and with all the strength, and to love his neighbour as himself, is more than all whole burnt offerings and sacrifices. (KJV)

Love is the essence of worship – when we love God, we praise and honour him. Love is also the basis for earthly life. It is as essential as food and water for meaningful survival. God's plan as unfolded in the Bible teaches us how to love Him and each other.

In a similar way, James 2:14-17 talks about faith:

> What good is it, my brothers, if a man claims to have faith but has no deeds? Can such faith save

him? Suppose a brother or sister is without clothes and daily food. If one of you says to him, 'Go, I wish you well; keep warm and well fed,' but does nothing about his physical needs, what good is it? In the same way, faith by itself, if it is not accompanied by action, is dead.

These strong words make it clear that faith is not simply a feeling or a wish, but is bound up in action. We can talk about the values we believe in, but true faith is demonstrated by deeds. If we care about the poor, we will find ways to help by donating time or money to a charity, or by providing a job or training to someone in need. We can choose to forgive those who have wronged us, and we can show love to those who are the hardest to love, but who need it the most. We can use our God-given skills and talents to make a positive difference in the communities where we are involved.

Regarding hope, Lamentations 3:19-22 says,

I remember my affliction and my wandering, the bitterness and the gall. I well remember them, and my soul is downcast within me. Yet this I call to mind and therefore I have hope: Because of the LORD's great love we are not consumed, for his compassions never fail.

Isn't it wonderful to know that no matter how difficult life may be, God will never abandon us? Family members grow distant or pass away. Friends move on or grow apart. But God does not change. No matter who we are or where we go, He has promised to always be with us. Nothing could be more reassuring than that! Any time of the day or night, wherever you are, and no matter the problem, God is just a prayer away and ready to respond when you turn to Him.

Romans 12:12 says,

> Be joyful in hope, patient in affliction, faithful in prayer.

These verses from Lamentations and Romans make it clear that we need to be proactive, to physically call to mind what we know to be true, and so remain joyfully hopeful. In other words, we should cultivate an underlying sense of hope, no matter our circumstances. We know that if God is for us, no one can stand against us. Each day brings our Heavenly Father's renewed grace. Ultimately, we should fear nothing, but rather rejoice in everything that God allows into our lives, as we know all things work together for the good of those who love Him and are called according to His purpose (Romans 8:28 paraphrased). Sometimes we need a reminder of our special status as God's chosen children. Nothing can separate us from the love of our King!

It is difficult to feel hopeful when a loved one receives a diagnosis of cancer, or you lose the job that supports your family. Many life situations feel like the opposite of joy. A recent news report indicates that the United States has the highest rates in the world of depression and anxiety. It is difficult to be carefree and joyful. But God promises believers that joy and hope are attainable and sustainable through faith.

FAITH, HOPE, AND LOVE ALL REQUIRE AN ELEMENT OF CHOICE

If we re-read the verses above, it becomes clear that there's an element of choice involved in all three of these important virtues. You can choose to believe, choose to love, and choose to be hopeful. In regard to choosing hope, Hebrews 10:23 says,

> Let us hold unswervingly to the hope we profess, for he who promised is faithful.

To 'hold unswervingly' is an individual choice and a commitment of faith. Faith, hope, and love work together synergistically to create a strong bond between us and God. Choosing hope must be based on a daily focus on renewal in response to God's everlasting love and grace:

> It is of the LORD's mercies that we are not consumed, because his compassions fail not. They are new every morning: great is thy faithfulness. The LORD is my portion, saith my soul; therefore, will I hope in him. The LORD is good unto them that wait for him, to the soul that seeketh him. It is good that a man should both hope and quietly wait for the salvation of the LORD. (Lamentations 3:22-26 KJV)

Of course, such a choice isn't always easy. In fact, sometimes making the right choice feels next to impossible. And yet, it's a choice that one of my fellow countrymen, Nelson Mandela, made again and again in extreme circumstances.

In his book, *Long Walk to Freedom*, he says,

> I am fundamentally an optimist. Whether that comes from nature or nurture, I cannot say. Part of being an optimist is keeping one's head pointed toward the sun, one's feet moving forward. There were many dark moments when my faith in humanity was sorely tested, but I would not and could not give myself up to despair. That way lays defeat and death.

Mandela's choice to remain hopeful is inspiring – and demonstrates the point that hope requires an element of choice. Imagine where South Africa might be today if he had chosen self-pity and bitterness instead of hope?

Though it is an intangible emotion, hope encourages action and inspires others. Although we don't have to keep busily engaged in mindless tasks for the sake of taking action, we can take productive steps toward securing our hope in the Lord and living a meaningful life that brings ourselves and others closer to Him. For some, that may require frequent Bible reading to discover what God is telling us. For others, getting involved in volunteer work or a particular ministry that they are passionate about might raise them to the next level of faith. Where are you in your spiritual journey? What might you physically do to live out and demonstrate your faith as bolstered by hope?

FAITH, HOPE, AND LOVE ALL HAVE A SPIRITUAL CONNECTION

1 John 4:7b-8 tells us,

> Everyone who loves has been born of God and knows God. Whoever does not love does not know God, because God is love.

These verses make it clear that God and love cannot be separated. God is the essence of love. He created love. He shares love with humans. All He asks is that we love Him in return, and love others around us. Love is the 'glue' that binds human hearts in a united relationship with our Creator.

In James 2:19 we read,

> You believe that there is one God. Good! Even the demons believe that – and shudder.

This verse leads us to understand that faith and belief are two different things. Belief is more about whether a person thinks something is real or not. Faith is about determining whether the object of belief can perform according to the promise made. For example, I believe in cars. But my faith in any individual car is based on the promise it makes in terms of safety, reliability, and stability (not to mention my faith – or otherwise – in the driver!). Therefore, in Christian terms, our faith isn't about whether we believe God is real, but whether we trust that He will fulfil the promises that He makes.

Regarding hope, Romans 15:13 says,

> May the God of hope fill you with all joy and peace as you trust in him, so that you may overflow with hope by the power of the Holy Spirit.

This verse tells us that God is the God of hope, and that hope comes from the Holy Spirit. Hope is also intertwined with faith. Faith in God leads to hope. A relationship with God is built on hope.

In summary, hope is both external and internal. It involves both choices and actions. It cannot be separated from our faith in God or from God Himself.

Over the course of this book we will take a much closer look at some factors that influence our outlook and feelings of hope. At the end of each chapter you'll find questions to ponder and answer. These will help you come to a better understanding of how you got to the point where you are now, and how you can move forward to flourish and enhance your relationship with God. This may require you to closely observe and analyse yourself and your situation – which may not be easy or comfortable. However, an honest look will reap rewards as you assess the status of your relationship with God and the level of hope on which your faith is built.

We need to start by having a look at the past. How have you arrived at a point where you are losing – or have lost – hope? Let's examine this question in terms of the core elements of hope discussed in this chapter.

QUESTIONS FOR REFLECTION

What external things have happened to you (e.g. events, insults, rejections, or grief) that have led to your current mindset?

_____
_____
_____

How would you describe your internal condition in terms of your sense of hope?

_____
_____
_____

What choices and actions – or lack of – have you taken/not taken that have made things worse for you?

_____
_____
_____

How would you describe your current relationship with God?

_____
_____
_____

CHAPTER TWO

MINDSET MATTERS

In Chapter One, we learned about the internal and intrinsically personal aspects of faith, hope, and love.

Although emotions should not entirely be relied upon as an accurate indication of what is true, faith, hope, and love are psychological impressions that we experience internally as feelings. Therefore, *they are influenced by what goes on in our hearts and minds*, and are, to some extent, *governed by our thoughts, attitudes, experiences, and opinions.*

Much of what happens in our lives is governed by what goes on in our heads – thoughts, attitudes, opinions, and how we view what happens to us through life experiences. In fact, because the mind is so important, several chapters in this book are dedicated to examining how various aspects of the way we think can influence our ability to hope and feel happy. We're going to start by looking at whether our fundamental ways of thinking are helping or hindering our sense of hope.

It's long been known that the mind is powerful. Some experts liken it to a biological computer that is capable of unfathomable calculations and functions. But do we always make the best use of it? Albert Einstein emphasised the importance of seeing and thinking clearly when he said,

'Small is the number of people who see with their eyes and think with their minds.' If this is true, it makes sense to take stock of how we are 'seeing' the world and consider whether we can look at our lives in a different way, in order to change our mindsets for the better.

From a Christian perspective, a key verse in Romans sheds light on the 'mental' aspect of faith. The first part of Romans 12:2 says,

> Do not conform any longer to the pattern of this world, but be transformed by the renewing of your mind.

Living differently comes about by thinking differently. We are who we are through who we *think* we are. We replace what we formerly thought of as important with an understanding of what is important in God's scheme of things. Interestingly, this new way of thinking releases a great spin-off, as described in the second part of the verse:

> Then you will be able to test and approve what God's will is – his good, pleasing and perfect will.

Doesn't that sound exciting? How often have you wondered what God's will is for your life? Has this knowledge generally seemed inaccessible? Perhaps you have believed that only the most spiritual people on earth or the most intelligent minds can determine God's will for the human race. Yet, Paul teaches that being transformed by the renewing of our minds allows each of us to 'test and approve' God's will – with the key shift being the process of mind transformation. This, therefore, adds to the case for spending some time looking at how we think. When we examine our thinking, we might be surprised at how much our thought patterns govern feelings of hope or positivity – for better or for worse. Our outlook on life, as well as the roadmap we follow, are shaped by thoughts that we allow or even encourage to dominate our minds and actions.

WHERE DO MINDSETS COME FROM?

When we arrive on this planet as babies, most of us come with an inbuilt desire to survive and an ability to learn. *What* we learn depends on when and where we are born, our parents' life experiences, our socio-economic circumstances, and our exposure to and indoctrination into a particular religious belief system – or none. These conditions of our birth, along with others, orient our life's direction. But many other aspects of daily life will become influential and guide our path throughout life. From infancy, through our school years and on through adulthood, marriage, and a career, many factors play a role in how we think about and relate to life and its meaning.

Personality, character, and IQ also play a role. Depending on the *type of person we are*, we will process what we see and hear and learn in a way that is unique to us as individuals. We are born with certain genetic traits that may predispose us to specific attitudes and behaviours. But many others are instilled through interactions with parents, siblings, friends, educators, employers, and others. As experience accumulates in our lives, we learn to react in ways that are influenced by how previous events and circumstances have made us feel about ourselves and the world around us, or in watching how others react to certain events.

FIONA'S STORY

Fiona was born in the 1960s and grew up in a middle-class, two-parent family in Wellington, New Zealand. She has an IQ that is above average. I'd describe her as a gentle person who avoids confrontation. In fact, she's likely to be the one to make peace if there are problems. With all the advantages that the time, place, and circumstances into which she was born gave her – together with a 'nice' personality – you would assume that her life would be relatively easy.

However, her mother (who was, in turn, a product of the environment she grew up in) had a rigid way of thinking and regarded parenting as the application of strict rules in order to make sure Fiona grew up well-behaved. Her mother also had the tendency to call Fiona 'useless' when she wasn't able to complete a task properly – even though it is natural to fail at things as you are growing up and learning new skills.

Fiona is far from useless. Yet, because she grew up hearing this message over and over, and because she has a gentle personality, she came to believe that she really was useless. *What* she learned, combined with the *type of person she is*, understandably resulted in her developing a negative mindset: 'If my parent thinks I'm useless, I must be useless.' In short, she felt bad about herself because of the authoritarian manner her mother used to train her daughter in a way that she felt was effective and needful.

This mindset of low self-esteem influenced Fiona's

decision-making as she grew up. Eventually she made bad choices. She started to look for love in the wrong places with the wrong people. She drank too much and allowed herself to be mistreated by others. Above all, she believed the life she was living was no better than a 'useless' person like her deserved. Her mother had delivered a strong message that continued to reverberate in Fiona's mind for years to come, overshadowing her self-image and shaping her attitude toward others.

You'll be pleased to know that Fiona's life began to turn around when she became a Christian. However, while the way Fiona's story unfolded as she grew up is unique to her, it isn't unique in terms of human experience. In fact, we all have stories about mindsets that were formed in our childhood days.

Some people grow up with an unclear idea of their origins or worth. Others are parented by dysfunctional people who lack the skills or commitment to nurturing a healthy family. Many, if not most, of us struggle with a variety of issues, while coming of age in homes and families that may grapple with challenges of their own. Trying to unravel all these influences to construct a meaningful and positive outlook can be overwhelming to achieve. Some individuals spend years in therapy trying to figure out who they are, what they believe, and what they want from life. Many others work through assorted problems that confuse their identity and life goals. Mental illness, addiction, and domestic conflicts further complicate the uncertainties of finding and maintaining a meaningful life journey. Some people wander through life and never quite figure out what they believe. They 'go with the flow' without thinking things through, led by the forceful and persuasive rhetoric of leaders – good or bad. When questioned about why they believe a certain way, they can't really explain it. Often, they will change their views as they realise there is no sound basis for their beliefs. Others continue to blindly follow others, often to their own loss or hurt.

But mindsets don't have to be negative; they can be positive, too. For example, values are part of our mindset. Most people are raised to value love, friendship, honesty, hard work, and good morals.

We are usually taught whether something is right or wrong. But these morals can vary. In one household, the pursuit of money via income, investments, or even gambling may be seen as important and 'right'. In another household, the love of money might be considered the root of all evil and therefore 'wrong'. Children tend to learn such lessons from parents without question. It's only as we get older – and gain perspective, education, and experience – that we begin to question these values and the rightness or wrongness of our mindset. We then begin to formulate opinions of our own, and choose our own paths and behaviours.

MINDSETS AND THINKING

Fiona's mindset affected the way she thought. And while becoming a Christian did transition her to a better path, she still took many of those old beliefs and values into her new life. Experience had taught her that bad things could, and did, happen – so much so that she came to expect trouble as being inevitable and just around the corner, rather than merely being aware that something unpleasant might possibly occur at some point down the road.

Fiona began to 'catastrophise' – a process where she automatically feared the worst. Her boss would ask to see her, and she would automatically conclude, 'I've done something wrong. I'm probably going to get fired.' Or, her husband might be delayed on his way home from work, and she would think, 'He's probably been in a car accident. Any minute now the police will arrive to tell me he's dead.' Such thoughts are stressful – but the stress felt is based on worst-case scenarios, not confirmed truth. Her mindset creates fear, which then imagines catastrophe. Fiona is very conscientious. The call to the boss's office could just as easily be to tell her that she's done a good job. Fiona's husband may have been delayed by traffic or a last-minute phone call before he left work for the day, but that's not the direction Fiona's thoughts took. She had been unconsciously trained to expect the worst in herself and in circumstances surrounding her, creating a cloud of gloom that followed wherever she went.

Anne Frank's thoughts took her in another direction. The young Jewish girl had plenty of reason to despair given that she and her family faced discovery as they hid from the Nazis in Amsterdam during World War II. Yet, in her posthumously published *The Diary of a Young Girl*, she wrote, '*I don't think of all the misery, but of the beauty that still remains.*' This positive mindset was no doubt sorely tested as grim events unfolded, but to be able to make such a positive statement when her life was in danger is a testament to the fact that she chose to 'see' the world in a positive light despite tremendous odds against a happy outcome. This shows that a person does not have to automatically assume the worst. In fact, it may be better to try to assume the best. Then, even when bad things occur, you will have remained calm and positive until the bad news is revealed.

MINDSETS ABOUT GOD

As Christians, we probably have a picture of God in our minds. By this, I don't mean an image of what God might look like. Rather, we think we know who God is by what we know and understand about Him, from the preaching and teaching of others, from reading the Bible, and from life experiences.

But do we really know God? How much of our understanding of God comes from what others have told us? Romans 11:33-36 says,

> O, the depth of the riches of the wisdom and knowledge of God! How unsearchable his judgments, and his paths beyond tracing out! Who has known the mind of the Lord? Or who has been his counsellor? Who has ever given to God, that God should repay him? For from him and through him and to him are all things.

In spite of these verses, many of us feel as though we know who God is and what He is like – and so our mindsets put both expectations and limitations on Him that might not be accurate. Sometimes, in limiting God, we also limit what He can do in and through us. Moses gives us a good example of this.

MOSES' STORY

On the face of it, many might consider Moses to be quite fortunate in his relationship with God. He 'saw' God in a way that most of us have not. He witnessed miraculous occurrences, had conversations with God, and experienced a specific call to undertake a specific task: he was to go to Pharaoh and appeal for the people of Israel to be released from Egypt. But Moses knew Pharaoh, having grown up in the Egyptian palace. He knew the enormity of the task. This made him question God's plan from the outset by coming up with multiple 'what if?' scenarios:

> [O Lord,] I have never been eloquent, neither in the past nor since you have spoken to your servant. I am slow of speech and tongue (Exodus 4:10).

Moses' mindset about who God was and what God could do meant that no signs, wonders, or reassurances were enough. And, when Moses had exhausted his list of 'what if?' scenarios, he turned the issue around and argued that he wasn't equipped for the task. Even when, in verse 11, God asks Moses, 'Who

Hope Rising

> gave man his mouth?... Is it not I, the LORD?' Moses says, 'O Lord, please send someone else to do it.'

MINDSETS AND HOPE

Looking at the way our mindsets affect the way we think and act, and even how we view God, illustrates the point: mindsets do matter. Not only that, but if your mindset is negative – and if your view of God is limiting – this will directly impact many areas of your life. This is most certainly true when it comes to hope. It's hard to hope if you're listening to internal messages of fear. It's hard to hope when your belief in God's ability to work on your behalf is small. It's hard to hope when you don't believe in yourself or others.

Remember, what you think is the truth may not be the truth. Your thoughts may be a mixture of the opinions, teachings, and values of others. It's important to take stock periodically and consider how your beliefs and ways of thinking may be influencing your life, your relationships, and your sense of hope. After all, mindset matters.

You probably know people with generally positive or negative mindsets. We should avoid those with negative mindsets. These are people who are too busy to carefully think things through. They mindlessly rush into danger or encourage others to do so. They expect every situation to turn out badly. When it does, they blame God or other people rather than themselves, even if they are the cause.

The positive ones are those you can go to for encouragement when you feel anxious, depressed, or uncertain.

They are people who model hope; their attitude reflects patience, trust, and optimism. But they don't offer false hope or meaningless platitudes like 'Everything will be fine' or 'There's no need to worry.' They recognise that life can be difficult but remind us that God is always with us and in control of the future. It is essential to remember this in order to remain calm and confident during times of upheaval in our lives. Someone with a positive outlook can put difficult things into perspective. They are not easily shaken. They offer a helping hand or a calm reminder. They know God and stay connected to Him. These are the people we turn to in times of stress and fear. Those are the people we need to become.

Positive people point us to God, whose wisdom is found in scriptures like Philippians 4:8:

> Finally, brethren, whatsoever things are true, whatsoever things *are* honest, whatsoever things *are* just, whatsoever things *are* pure, whatsoever things *are* lovely, whatsoever things *are* of good report; if *there be* any virtue, and if *there be* any praise, think on these things.

Questions for Reflection

How have your attitudes and mindset affected the way you view the external things (e.g. events, insults, rejections or grief) that have happened to you?

_____
_____
_____

How have your mindset and way of thinking impacted your current internal state in terms of your sense of hope?

_____
_____
_____

How has your mindset influenced the actions you have taken or significant choices you have made in the past?

_____
_____
_____

How do these mindsets continue to influence the actions you take or the choices you make today?

_____
_____
_____

Mindset Matters

In what way do you think that your current relationship with God is negatively impacted by your mindset about Him, and – like Moses – what you think of yourself and your ability to rise above a difficult situation?

_____
_____
_____

What practical steps could you take to change your mindset and impact your level of hope for the better?

_____
_____
_____

One Last Thing

If, like Fiona, you suffer from negative automatic thinking that undermines your sense of hope, please don't assume your situation can't be improved. You can train yourself to overcome such thought processes. Next time you find yourself thinking in such a way, try the following technique (based on cognitive behaviour therapy):

1. Write a brief summary of the situation that has made you think negatively (e.g. my boss wants to see me).

   _____
   _____
   _____

2. Note a few words that describe how the situation is making you feel (e.g. panic, fear, dread, guilt).

_____
_____
_____

3. Identify your key negative thought (e.g. I am going to get fired).

_____
_____
_____

4. List evidence to support this negative thought. (e.g. people do lose their jobs for being incompetent. My boss has high standards.)

_____
_____
_____

5. Write the evidence against this negative thought. (e.g. I work really hard. I'm never late. I go the extra mile. I try to be considerate of others. One of the other bosses told me I did a good job last week.)

_____
_____
_____

6. Now try to replace the negative thought with an alternative that is more truthful. (e.g. I have no reason to assume the call to see my boss is bad news. I have done my best and have nothing to worry about.)

_____

_____

_____

If you use this technique every time you start thinking negatively, you will soon find that you can rewire your mind and stop yourself from going straight to the worst-case scenario. You can begin to replace negative thoughts with more positive and hopeful ones.

CHAPTER THREE
Entitlement and Expectation

Western society is built on positive elements, such as education, healthcare, housing, transport, and technology. Many people in Western countries are able to access these and related programs to make their lives more convenient and comfortable. Many become better educated, consult doctors if they are unwell, and move beyond the boundaries of the neighbourhood where they grew up if they choose. They can rent or buy a house that's far grander than dwellings in developing nations, and they may even be able to travel to see the world for business or pleasure, visiting new cultures and absorbing different ideas. Imported foods, luxury cars, and quality education are widely available, while government assistance is available for those who need it.

Technology has greatly improved our lives. We can be kept up to date with world events in an instant through social media or the internet's broad access to many types of programs, websites, and apps, and we can communicate with people on the other side of the planet as though they were just next door. We can be medically examined and diagnosed with precision. We can cook faster, wash clothes more easily, be informed more quickly, and entertain ourselves with games, books and movies, along with a host of online content.

On the other hand, rates of chronic disease, mental illness, and even poverty are growing by the day. Rather than finding that the advantages of Western society make life better, many people are becoming increasingly stressed, isolated, lonely, depressed, anxious, or just plain dissatisfied. Even boredom is on the rise! The rich get richer, but the Western poor find themselves more marginalised, penalised, and disenfranchised by the day. The government's welfare programs are constantly re-evaluated and updated to meet the growing need of people who are unemployed or underemployed. Most people complain of being 'time poor' – or they fill up the spare time they do have with pursuits that are addictive but ultimately pointless. Social media, entertainment, and gambling devour time and money that leave many people poor in both pocket and wisdom. These days, far more people consume than create.

Furthermore, many items once seen as luxuries are now viewed as necessities. Nowadays it's difficult to live in Western society without a computer, a smartphone, and internet access. Many families acquire several televisions and computers, as well as more than one vehicle, along with countless clothing articles, grooming aids, and recreational toys. So, we buy these 'necessities' and feel momentarily satisfied. But modern technology isn't built to last. Even if you don't have a desire for the latest and greatest, most electronic devices are lucky to last five years before they start malfunctioning and need to be replaced. Within that period, many people become even more attached to the device, some to the point of addiction, resulting in an obsessive 'need' for these items that just a generation ago did not even exist – and people got along just fine without them. Conveniences that were once seen as 'labour-saving' devices instead seem to consume time or, worse, are so labour-saving that technology makes someone's former job a task no longer requiring human input.

On top of this, extensive exposure to what's available just about anywhere on credit at high interest rates makes many people want more and more and more. In fact, it's not just a 'want' any more, nor is it a need. Rather, it's a strange compulsion to keep up and fit in with what we are told are the most desirable possessions or looks or attitudes. We willingly settle under the yoke of financial burden to create a façade of wealth that is not real and cannot last – mainly to impress people who neither know us nor care about what we have or don't have. Anxiety creeps in as we wonder whether we have finally become 'cool' enough or cultivated enough to be viewed as acceptable by peers. That anxiety increases when the monthly credit card balances start growing to the point where we run up a credit balance to pay off a previous credit balance, becoming enmeshed in ever-growing debt without sustained satisfaction.

We project our chosen image to others via social media to make an impression that will attract the desired results. These games involving masks and charades are time-consuming and, ultimately, meaningless, as King Solomon mused during his rule as revealed in Ecclesiastes 1:2 (KJV):

> Vanity of vanities, saith the Preacher, vanity of vanities; all is vanity.

It can be exhausting, and it all results in a skewed mindset – entitlement.

The word 'entitle' is defined in the *Oxford Dictionary* as 'to give a right or just claim to.' Therefore, *entitlement is when a person claims the right for* something. It's a fitting word for many Western people today: they feel they are entitled to so much more than they currently possess. And, it's a message that's reinforced on a daily basis by marketing gurus, self-fulfilment advocates, and even prosperity preachers. Society continually reminds us that we deserve the biggest and best of everything.

Such messaging is conveyed in many different ways.

Children can be raised with the idea that the world is their oyster. They are encouraged to dream big and are told that nothing is impossible. Even Walt Disney, the creator of a sort of modern magic, allegedly said, '*If you can dream it, you can do it.*' While some children are probably still raised with a 'this is as good as it's going to get for you' message, the majority hear the opposite. Parents, after all, usually want something better for their children than they had themselves. But, even in today's world, is everything really attainable? And, even if dreams can become reality, is the path to claim them reliably smooth, or is it strewn with various obstacles? How far will we go and to what depths will we sink to grab what we want?

There is nothing wrong with nurturing a dream and pursuing it wholeheartedly. A meaningful quest can stir embers of hope and set it ablaze in the hearts of those determined to succeed. Great things have been accomplished by great minds who remain committed to achieving quality dreams. However, it is unwise to encourage someone to chase a dream that will never materialise. Failure to reach the goal creates disappointment, and disappointment often leads to bitterness. Parents can sometimes rush to make everything okay for their children rather than allowing them to learn how to overcome setbacks. Everyone should learn how to deal with failure without losing hope.

The message of entitlement is also reinforced through advertising. We are bombarded with daily prompts, both obvious and subtle, that try to raise the bar on our quality of life. Such messaging tells us we can't possibly live well or be happy if we don't look or smell a certain way, don't drive a certain car or own a certain thing. A corresponding underlying message suggests that we don't just *need* this stuff in order to fit in, we *deserve* it. It is our right.

Even Western Christian teaching and preaching can promote a false sense of entitlement. For instance, let's consider what's often referred to as the 'prosperity doctrine'. Teachers of the prosperity doctrine tell us that, in exchange for Christians having faith in God, living 'good' lives, and donating money to the church, God will bless us financially, ensure good health, and provide safety and security. Some teachers or preachers back up this idea with verses of Scripture to justify their message. And many people accept this teaching as gospel. If a single verse tells us we deserve great things, it must be true – and false teachers then feel entitled to receive such promises by distorting God's Word out of context to meet their material desires while encouraging their flock to have the same expectations.

The result of all these messages of entitlement is that our expectations are raised. We count on our desires being satisfied without putting much hope or effort into them.

'Expectation' is defined in the *Oxford Dictionary* in this way:

1. expecting, looking forward with hope or fear, etc; and
2. what one expects; the probability (of an event); the probable duration (of life); prospects of an inheritance.

Notice the mention of the word 'hope' in this definition. While we can expect with fear, many people expect with hope. And, because hope is linked to expectation, it's very important to take a look at our expectations in three ways:

- Consider whether what we expect is realistic.
- Analyse whether our unrealistic expectations are causing us to lose hope.
- Determine how our expectation impacts our overall faith in God.

REALISTIC EXPECTATIONS

When considering whether what we expect is realistic, a better approach might be to consider whether what we expect is scriptural. We need to make sure we have a strong relationship with God and an understanding of His truth as explained in the Bible. God's ways often run counter to those of humanity.

It's important for us to consider how verses of Scripture fit into the Bible as a whole rather than taking random verses here or there and seizing upon them as being a reflection of that whole. We need our view of God to be as complete as humanly possible rather than just being mere fragments of a complex puzzle. Sadly, some Christians reduce God to something He is not. God is mighty and

Entitlement and Expectation

powerful, awesome and majestic. He isn't simply the great 'car-park-finder' in the sky or a kind vending machine for our earthly wants. Let's look at some things we can truthfully expect from God:

WE CAN EXPECT GOD'S LOVE
1 John 4:16 tells us,

> And so we know and rely on the love God has for us. God is love. Whoever lives in love lives in God, and God in him.

This is a beautiful promise, one that is made complete in our salvation through faith in the Lord Jesus. This is an expectation we can rely on when we trust in God's salvation for us through Jesus's death on the cross and resurrection from the grave. This does not mean we can do or must do anything to merit salvation. Jesus has done it all – paid the price for every human being – through His life, death, and resurrection. To accept this wondrous gift, all we have to do is believe in and follow Him.

WE CAN EXPECT GOD'S JUSTICE
We learn from Romans 12:19:

> Do not take revenge, my friends, but leave room for God's wrath, for it is written: 'It is mine to avenge; I will repay,' says the Lord.

If you have been mistreated by others, this verse might be an encouragement as you picture God righting wrongs on your behalf. But God's justice may take an unexpected turn that differs from human ideas. And don't forget the following verse (Romans 12:20):

> If your enemy is hungry, feed him; if he is thirsty, give him something to drink. In doing this, you will heap burning coals on his head.

God wants us to forgive, just as we have been forgiven by Him. He is a God of love before He is a God of wrath. If you are putting your hope in God to bring justice, you need to realise that God's plan is about forgiveness and reconciliation. For justice is bound up in forgiveness, as we read in 1 John 1:9:

> If we confess our sins, he is faithful and *just* and will forgive us our sins and purify us from all unrighteousness.

Therefore, we can expectantly receive forgiveness and also anticipate that God will be the determiner of where justice should fall at the end of all things. We are not entitled to anything else except His mercy, and that only by His gracious love.

WE CAN EXPECT GOD TO BE INTERESTED IN OUR FUTURE

A verse that is much quoted is Jeremiah 29:11:

> 'For I know the plans I have for you,' declares the LORD, 'plans to prosper you and not to harm you, plans to give you hope and a future.'

Many Christians find this verse a great encouragement, and they 'hope' for the prosperity promised here. But Scripture also says other things about the future. For example, Solomon, in Ecclesiastes 8:5-6, emphasises the role of wisdom:

> Whoever obeys his command will come to no harm, and the wise heart will know the proper time and procedure. For there is a proper time and procedure for every matter, though a man's misery weighs heavily upon him.

And in Isaiah 45:7 we learn more about God:

> I form the light and create darkness,
> I bring prosperity and create disaster;
> I, the LORD, do all these things.

If we only focus on the verse from Jeremiah 29, we might form the expectation that God's plans for our future are going to be 'good' and that prosperity will soon abound. We glean a picture of what prosperity might look like, and we project that image onto God's will for the future. But the other two verses help us to understand that events must happen at the proper time, and our God of love will sometimes allow trouble to come our way. We'll explore this subject more in Chapter Six, but, for now, realise this: we can expect God to be interested in our future, but we are not entitled for that future to be completely rosy and exactly how we want it to be. If this is what you expect but isn't what you get, you may find you lose hope and that your faith in God starts to waver.

Why wouldn't the future be rosy? Doesn't God want His children to be happy? God loves us, His children, and often gives us many wonderful gifts. But being wise, He does not merely satisfy our demands and desires. He trains us to be more like Him when we submit to His will for our lives.

Be assured that God has a life-long plan for you, and He will also provide the means to fulfil it.

WE CAN EXPECT GOD'S PROVISION

Jesus explained God's provision in this way (Matthew 6:25-26):

> Therefore, I tell you, do not worry about your life, what you will eat or drink; or about your body, what you will wear. Is not life more important than food, and the body more important than clothes? Look at the birds of the air; they do not sow or reap or store away in barns, and yet your heavenly Father feeds them. Are you not much more valuable than they?

What's interesting about these two verses is that they focus not so much on provision but on attitude – having a grasp on what is really important. God does not want us to think about *what* we might receive, but rather *that* we will receive it.

This teaching is backed by what James has to say:

> You do not have, because you do not ask God. When you ask, you do not receive, because you ask with wrong motives, that you may spend what you get on your pleasures. (James 4:2-3)

Entitlement and Expectation

So, in terms of expectation, we know that God will provide for us. However, we should not expect that entitlement will extend to extras we don't need. God wants us to focus on what's important, not on what isn't.

Those distinctions between 'want' and 'need' can be surprising. We might believe a job pay raise is needed in order to meet financial obligations each month. But God may prefer to withhold a pay raise until we learn to responsibly manage what He has already provided through current income. We know as believers that God always provides for His children in one way or another. But we don't know exactly what to expect, or when. That's okay. As long as we trust God and follow His leading, everything will work out for our good and God's glory.

THE IMPACT OF UNREALISTIC EXPECTATIONS

To illustrate the impact of unrealistic expectations, let's take a look at the story of Jonah in the Bible.

JONAH'S STORY

The prophet Jonah is famous for being swallowed by a 'great fish', likely a whale or similar species. However, although most of us will never end up in the belly of a sea creature, there's much we can learn from Jonah about both entitlement and expectation.

At the beginning of the story, God calls Jonah to go to the great city of Nineveh to 'preach against it, because its wickedness has come up before me' (Jonah 1:2).

Jonah isn't keen on this plan because, like us, he undoubtedly prefers to avoid evil rather than confront it. He runs away to sea and gets on a ship headed in the opposite direction. The vessel and crew are caught up in a storm so fierce that it causes the sailors to cast lots to find out the reason for the tempest. When the lots indicate that Jonah is the cause of the maelstrom, they reluctantly agree to throw him into the sea, where he's swallowed by a large fish. Terrified, Jonah prays for salvation and promises to make good on his call to Nineveh. At God's command, the fish then vomits Jonah onto dry land.

Keeping his word, Jonah travels to Nineveh and proclaims God's message: 'Forty more days and Nineveh will be overturned.' Jonah 3:5 tells us,

> The Ninevites believed God. They declared a fast and, all of them, from the greatest to the least, put on sackcloth.

Many preachers and prophets would be thrilled with such an outcome! God expresses His delight in chapter 3, verse 10:

> When God saw what they did and how they turned from their evil ways, he had compassion and did not bring upon them the destruction he had threatened.

But Jonah's response did not mirror the Lord's. Instead, we are told, 'Jonah was greatly displeased and became angry.' His anger focused on the fact that God had changed His plan and did not do as He had threatened. Jonah wanted to see Nineveh burn. He was so angry that he complained to God, 'Now, O Lord, take away my life, for it is better for me to die than to live.'

Jonah then stormed off in a huff and made himself a shelter while he waited to see what would happen to the city. That's some reaction – one that's all the more notable because we are told that Jonah knew God's character:

> I knew that you are a gracious and compassionate God, slow to anger and abounding in love, a God who relents from sending calamity. (Jonah 4:2)

What motivated Jonah's outburst? Did he feel he would suffer personal humiliation when God failed to come through with the promised wrath? Did he expect to have that 'I told you so' moment in front of any Ninevites who made it out alive? Did he feel a sense of entitlement to know what God had intended all along?

The Book of Jonah does not make the prophet's underlying reasons clear. What we do learn is that, in the face of dashed expectations, Jonah behaved like a spoilt child who doesn't get its way. Jonah laid the blame for his expectations of God – and for his own sense of entitlement – not on himself, but on God.

What's significant about God's reaction to Jonah's tantrum is that He's as compassionate to Jonah as He had been with the Ninevites. We read in Jonah 4:6,

> Then the Lord God provided a vine and made it grow up over Jonah to give shade for his head to ease his discomfort, and Jonah was very happy about the vine.

Although God subsequently took the vine away in order to further mature Jonah's character, I love this picture of God extending compassion in order to give Jonah time to adjust his thinking and to understand that in God's agenda, Jonah wasn't entitled to expect anything of God other than graciousness and love. Because, at the end of the day, Jonah's anger was the direct outcome of unrealistic expectations. God's object lessons, using first the great fish and then a natural vine, reveal the points that Jonah needed to grasp about God's nature, and his own.

Expectations and Faith

The story of Jonah not only illustrates the way in which unrealistic expectations impact our moods and outlook, but also how expectations can affect our faith. We see this from the very beginning of the book when we watch Jonah's response

Entitlement and Expectation

to God's call: he flees. Why does he do this? Is it because he'd rather do something else, or he's uninterested – or afraid? Does he struggle with obedience, as most of us do?

Whatever Jonah's reasoning, he doesn't see God's call as a privilege or an honour. He also doesn't appear to consider God as someone he can rely on to help him get the task done. Both at the beginning of his quest and at its conclusion, Jonah had to learn some difficult lessons. His understanding of God's nature continued to expand. Sometimes we experience similar thoughts and emotions today. We often put our faith in worldly things, like prosperity or relationships, rather than in God. Is this because our visionary expectations of God are too small? Or do we not understand that God just wants us to be willing and available, and that,

> The one who calls you is faithful and he will do it? (1 Thessalonians 5:24)

Can you see the connection between your feelings of entitlement, your expectations, and your sense of hope? How you see your life and how you understand God has an effect on how you think, how you act, and, ultimately, how you feel. You may well be putting your hope in things you are not entitled to – and end up having your hopes dashed when expectations are not met.

Hope Rising

QUESTIONS FOR REFLECTION

When external things (e.g. events, insults, rejections, or grief) have happened to you, what has been your internal reaction? Have you believed that you deserved better or that life isn't fair? Or, if you have been blessed with good things, have you been grateful or felt you'd received what was due to you?

_____

_____

_____

How have your reactions to external circumstances impacted your internal state in terms of your sense of hope and the goodness of God?

_____

_____

_____

In what ways have your feelings of entitlement or your unrealistic expectations influenced past actions or choices?

_____

_____

_____

What actions or choices are you making right now as a result of feelings of entitlement or unrealistic expectations?

Entitlement and Expectation

In what ways could you change your behaviour and choices for the better?

_____

_____

_____

In what ways do you think that your current relationship with God is being negatively impacted by your feelings of entitlement or unrealistic expectations? Can you say you really know or understand God's plan and purposes for your life? If not, what can you do to enhance that understanding?

_____

_____

_____

CHAPTER FOUR

Updating Your Understanding

Hindsight is a wonderful thing. It's that moment of clarity when you see the big picture; where you finally know and understand – or gain wisdom about – events that have gone before. It's the moment of transition between stumbling along as though blind to receiving clearer sight.

What's not so wonderful are the bits that occur before we gain hindsight – the bits where we struggle and slog and suffer; where we pray for relief or for an explanation from God about what the heck is going on with our lives. Stumbling around in a mental fog is not enjoyable on any level. But sometimes it is a necessary step or two on the path to enlightenment.

In times of trouble, hope can seem to be in short supply. This may cause us to doubt others, doubt ourselves and, most particularly, doubt God. We wrestle with the idea that somewhere, within the chaos, there must be a plan. God must surely know what He's doing. Why doesn't He explain? Why is He asking this of me? Why do I have to go through this? Why isn't there a shortcut?

Why, why, why, why?

It's a fair question, isn't it? We feel that we *should* know what God is up to, that God *should* give us an explanation.

After all, an updated understanding of what God is doing is surely vital if we're to be effective Christians. Even a few spiritual hints would help.

And yet, when you think about it, questioning God about what He's up to is another sort of doubt, or entitlement. This entitlement says, 'It's my life you're playing with. The very least you could do is give me an explanation.' But, like all entitlements, we need to consider this thought carefully and examine it in light of what Scripture teaches. We need to consider, 'Should we ask the reason why? Are we entitled to know the answers?'

In fact, asking *why* is sometimes neither helpful nor hopeful. Let's look at this more closely.

WANTING TO KNOW WHY IS WHAT GOT US INTO TROUBLE IN THE FIRST PLACE

In the Garden of Eden, when making his pitch for why Eve should eat the forbidden fruit, the serpent says,

> For God knows that when you eat of it your eyes will be opened, and you will be like God, knowing good and evil. (Genesis 3:5)

Such attractive language is irresistible – the idea of having your eyes opened and being *like God*. Certainly, the temptation appealed enough to Eve and then Adam that they were prepared to disobey their Creator and do the one thing they had been told not to do.

When you think about it in these terms, asking *why* is the same thing. The only difference is that we are directly asking God to open our eyes so that we can know what He knows. We seek the forbidden fruit of hidden knowledge that would make us more like God.

For whatever reason – and there are probably some good ones – God does not want us to know all that He knows. Knowledge is power, and God is all-powerful. But humans are not supposed to be as powerful as God or equal with Him.

For a start, if we knew everything, we'd have little or no reason to depend on God. As soon as we know something, we have a tendency to take matters into our own hands – to try to change course and slow down or speed up the process in a way that seems best to us. Such manipulation may, in fact, take us away from the path that God intended. Sadly, we tend to maintain a self-centred attitude about the future. We want life to be good for us. What we cannot know is how the current situation, circumstances, and even the location of our lives on this planet impacts, interacts with, or counterbalances the lives of others and what God is trying to do in the grander scheme. We need to remind ourselves that everything isn't about us, that there is a time and season for all things, and that God's plan encompasses the universe, not just our finite space.

In short, if God wanted us to know, He would have given us that knowledge.

WANTING TO KNOW WHY IS OFTEN POINTLESS

God has made it clear from the beginning that He does not intend us to have full knowledge of His works. What makes us think He's going to change His mind just because we want answers? Wringing our hands and asking 'Why?' is, therefore pointless.

However, one day we *will* know. Paul says in 1 Corinthians 13:12,

> Now we see but a poor reflection as in a mirror; then we shall see face to face. Now I know in part; then I shall know fully, even as I am fully known.

Therefore, we need to have faith that God knows what He's doing, and be content to let Him rule. We need to realise there are reasons for our difficulties, but that we won't know those reasons until later. The verse above comes right before the very first verse quoted in this book:

> And now these three remain: faith, hope and love. But the greatest of these is love. (1 Corinthians 13:13)

Love is the most powerful emotion we can experience that will guide us through whatever situations we may encounter. God is love; we love Him because He first loved us. Engulfed in that love and bolstered by it, we can face anything this world can throw at us by maintaining our hold on Jesus as our rock of salvation. That is hope.

ASKING 'WHY' IS DANGEROUS

It's easy to assume that it would be helpful to acquire God-like knowledge of the future. Humans have craved this knowledge for generations. If you knew your future career path or who you would marry, you could avoid wasting time or heading in the wrong direction. However, that something *may* happen is quite different from *how* these things come to pass. All sorts of learning experiences may be needed before you are ready to step into your future path. As stated earlier in this book, it is worth repeating that you might need to develop in more specific ways as a certain kind of person before you can become potential healthy spouse material, for example, or before taking on the role God intends for you.

SARAH'S STORY

In Genesis, the first book of the Bible, we read of Abram and Sarai (later renamed Abraham and Sarah). Even though Abraham and Sarah were childless and advanced in years, God promised Abraham that his offspring would be as numerous as the stars. Abraham creditably believed this promise, but Sarah thought the promise was far-fetched. After all, her childbearing days were behind her. So, she manipulated the situation by giving Abraham her Egyptian maidservant, Hagar. Her manipulation worked, to a degree. Hagar became pregnant and, subsequently, gave birth to a son named Ishmael.

Yet, in the fullness of time, against all odds, Sarah did become pregnant, through the ways and means God intended, and Isaac was born. But Ishmael remained a thorn in Sarah's side. In Genesis 21:9-10 we read:

> But Sarah saw that the son whom Hagar the Egyptian had borne to Abraham was mocking, and she said to Abraham, 'Get rid of that slave woman and her son, for that slave woman's son

will never share in the inheritance with my son Isaac.'

Sarah's request distressed Abraham, but God assured him that Ishmael would be looked after and become the father of a nation, just as Isaac would. Then, the half-brothers, Isaac and Ishmael, were parted and never again joined together. The two people groups that descended from these men remain divided to this day – a tragedy that might have been avoided had Sarah not tried to fulfil in her own way the promise God had given Abraham and her.

WANTING TO KNOW WHY LOOKS AROUND RATHER THAN UP

As defined earlier, hope is the expectation and desire for a certain event to occur. Ultimately, hope looks forward. Asking why something did not work out as planned provides the opportunity to reflect on events that occurred and then learn from them. While, as we have seen, there are times when it is important to turn from the past as we face the future and learn from where we've been, sometimes we get stuck in the past. Thus, it is important not to wallow in losses or failures, but rather to learn from them and keep moving forward.

The question to ask is this: Can a person look backward and forward at the same time?

Perhaps not simultaneously, but possibly consecutively. It's about having wisdom to decide when to look back, but not live there. Remember, hope and faith are interlinked with trust, and all three should motivate us to move forward. God has a plan, and it is up to us to identify it and embrace it.

ASKING WHY CAN LEAD TO DARK PLACES

Before moving forward, we need to look again at some things we've learned up to this point. We have seen that our attitudes and mindsets about God and our beliefs about our entitlements all work together to influence our outlook and levels of hope. This picture is further complicated by our expectations in the areas of love, justice, the future, provision, and faith. All these components have a huge bearing on *how* we look at life, *what* we expect, and *why* we expect it.

If life fails to live up to our expectation of entitlement, it's probably not surprising that we will start to ask, 'Why?' Many have asked that question (although usually only when things go wrong!), and there are only three possible outcomes to such a question:

1. God provides an answer – and we are either satisfied or dissatisfied with His response. However, such answers are rare, because, in general, that's not how God works.
2. No answer manifests – in which case we will continue to wrestle with the question, and probably continue to ask the question over and over.
3. Eventually an answer appears. Further down the track, as we mature and grow, we come to see the answer, and hindsight dawns on our understanding.

However, since number one is rare, and number three takes time, we are often left with response number two. We get no answer and continue to ask 'Why?' If the negative events, insults, rejections, or grief persist long enough, bitterness and resentment set in. And, if combined with misplaced feelings of entitlement or expectation, getting to bitterness and resentment might not take long.

Of all the negative human emotions, bitterness and resentment are possibly the most dangerous. They are dark, not of God, and frequently lead to hatred and a desire for revenge. Bitterness and resentment are about as far away from hope as you can get. The Bible reminds us not to hold on to negative emotions, especially toward others. We are to have the mind of Christ toward all things and people – not always easy, but God provides the means and incentives if we agree to follow through.

In many ways, humans are selfish. We want what we want – and when we want it! So, when we ask God for something that we feel sure is within His divine will, we often become perplexed and then angry when He doesn't grant it right away or in the way we think He should. We know God loves each of us. We trust that He loves marriage and hates divorce, as indicated in the Bible. Why then does He not heal broken marriages? We know that Jesus has a tender heart for young children – so why does He permit them to suffer chronic illness and sometimes die? We know the Bible teaches us to be self-supporting by an honest trade, so why does He not provide jobs for those who need them?

As Job discovered, there are no easy answers when questioning God. In fact, Job soon learned it is never wise to question God. Our Creator has a plan and a promise for each person's life. It is up to us to focus on our personal life journey and to stay faithful to God's calling and teaching. Getting angry or disappointed in God will only create roadblocks to our journey.

WANTING TO KNOW WHY CAN UNDERMINE YOUR FAITH IN GOD

In all likelihood, asking 'why?' may undermine your faith in God. Remember, Hebrews 11:1 defines faith as

> being sure of what we hope for and certain of what we do not see.

With faith, we do not need to ask why; we simply need to trust – trust that the object of our faith can perform according to the promises made. We must have confidence that God knows what He's doing. While simple, childlike faith is not easy, we can work to rediscover it by spending quality time in God's presence, becoming familiar with the Bible, waiting on Him, and praying patiently for direction and guidance.

Earlier, we looked at Jeremiah 29:11:

> 'For I know the plans I have for you,' declares the LORD, 'plans to prosper you and not to harm you, plans to give you a future and a hope.'

However, while this verse is often quoted, the subsequent verses are not – which is unfortunate because they are equally important. Verses 12 and 13 state:

> Then you will call upon me and come and pray to me, and I will listen to you. You will seek me and find me when you seek me with all your heart.

The next time you're tempted to ask *why*, consider whether it's the best question to be asking – and whether, by doing so, you are undermining your sense of hope. There is a time to ask questions and to seek information as well as a time to wait for God's revelation.

QUESTIONS FOR REFLECTION

When external setbacks (e.g. events, insults, rejections, or grief) have happened to you, what has been your reaction? Have you asked 'Why?' What insights did you gain? What negative effects did you experience?

_____

_____

_____

_____

How has your desire to know the answers impacted your internal state regarding a sense of hope?

_____

_____

_____

_____

In what way has your lack of understanding about what God intends for you influenced your actions or choices?

_____

_____

_____

_____

Hope Rising

How are your current actions and choices being influenced by a lack of understanding as to what God intends for you?

_____
_____
_____
_____

In what way do you think your current relationship with God is negatively impacted by a need to know why?

_____
_____
_____
_____

CHAPTER FIVE

MIGHTY IS OUR MASTER

As we have seen, it's easy to fall into the trap of asking 'why?' as we try to make sense of our personal experiences and the events of our lives. But people don't just ask this question for themselves. They also want to know what God is up to in a universal sense. Why does God allow suffering? Why doesn't God just *do* something to make things right?

As Christians, we are not immune to asking such questions, and sometimes we are put on the spot by others asking those questions of us. There are no easy answers, so we struggle to respond. That feeling of uncertainty leaves us unsettled. This can, in turn, chip away at the foundations of our faith and, consequently, our hope.

The truth is that we really don't know the plans of God – and that's where faith is required. As we mature, we can learn to live with not having all the answers. The bottom line is that God knows what He's doing – even if we don't. But I think there is one possible explanation, which lies in the concept of freedom of choice.

If you look at the story of creation in Genesis, the placement of the tree of the knowledge of good and evil is an interesting move on the part of God. After all, if the tree hadn't been there, the Fall wouldn't have happened, and the disconnection between God and us wouldn't exist.

So why was the tree placed there?

A possible explanation is that the tree provided choice. Because, if you think about it, without the tree, what choice did Adam and Eve have except to love God? And as we know very well in our modern world, which values both freedom and personal choice so highly, a lack of choice is restrictive and frustrating. We consider it unfair, even. Denied choices can lead to bitterness and resentment. And, at its most extreme, the removal of freedom of choice can lead to a servitude mindset that gnaws at our feelings of joy and trust in our Creator.

Freedom of choice is good, but it comes with consequences. People will exercise their free will in all sorts of ways, both for the greater good and for selfish purposes. We have centuries of history attesting to the ways in which people have exercised freedom of choice, sometimes with dire outcomes. Often, people did not mean for their actions to negatively impact others, and were aghast when that happened. Other times, people didn't care if their actions harmed the innocent as long as they got their way.

You may have first-hand experience of this. Part of the reason you have ended up in the situation you're in right now may have its roots in the bad choices of others. Parents, employers, or even strangers may have made decisions or taken action in ways that intentionally or accidentally affected you. Car accidents and theft are two examples of damaging choices. Or, current circumstances may be a result of your own choices – or a combination of both. Either way, the consequences of bad decisions can be temporarily or permanently devastating. If only we, and others, had paused to count the cost before grabbing what we felt was more important than anything or anyone else.

Adam and Eve's choice of disobedience has had two serious repercussions: humanity's relationship with God was broken, and their actions have resulted in events, calamities, and grief that are not of God's making. People often end up blaming God for tragic outcomes that are actually the consequences of the bad choices of human beings. God restricted neither our freedom to make choices, nor the natural consequences that would follow.

So, why doesn't God intervene? Perhaps one reason is that to do so would remove our freedom to choose. Would we all become slaves or robots? Would we resent God for denying us the option of choosing for ourselves whom we will serve?

If you think about it, to be Christian is to make a choice – an eternal decision. We choose a relationship with God and receive forgiveness of sin along with everlasting salvation. We put ourselves in the hands of the Lord and say, as Jesus did,

> Yet not as I will, but as you will. (Matthew 26:39)

This is a deeply entrenched decision that affects us in every possible way – physically, psychologically, and spiritually, both now and forever. It also has the potential to affect countless others in our lives or who observe us in public life. Becoming a Christian sets us apart from the world, although we continue to live in it without being part of it.

At the outset, this may be a decision with consequences you don't fully understand – you might not have a complex understanding of what being a Christian entails. You simply hear God's call and respond to it, knowing that forgiveness and salvation are needed as much as oxygen, and actually more so, because these gifts transcend physical existence to permeate our eternal being. Simple faith can be beautiful and lasting. It gives us peace and security. Jesus taught that we should have faith like a child.

Yet, as our emotional relationship with the Lord grows and develops, so also should our knowledge and understanding of God and His ways. 1 Peter 2:2 tells us:

> Like new born babies, crave spiritual milk, so that by it you may grow up in your salvation.

In 1 Corinthians 3:2-3, Paul tells the believers of Corinth,

> I gave you milk, not solid food, for you were not yet ready for it. Indeed, you are still not ready. You are still worldly. For since there is jealousy and quarrelling among you, are you not worldly? Are you not acting like mere men?

Like the Corinthians, we need to examine ourselves and ask whether we are still worldly, and whether we are still acting like mere men or women. Part of the readiness Paul refers to is understanding our place as Christians from God's perspective – for in living where God wants us to be (as citizens of His kingdom on earth), in the way that God wants us to live (as His loving disciples), we will find the hope we so desperately desire.

Our readiness to be part of God's world lies in understanding the might and sovereignty of the Father. Paul explains the distinction between God the Son and God the Father in Romans 8:31-34:

> What, then, shall we say in response to this? If God is for us, who can be against us? He who did not spare his own Son, but gave him up for us all – how will he not also, along with him, graciously give us all things? Who will bring any charge against those whom God has chosen? It is God who justifies. Who is he that condemns? Christ Jesus, who died – more than that, who was raised to life – is at the right hand of God and is interceding for us.

In our relationship with God the Son (Jesus), we are invited to think of Him as both Lord and Saviour, and brother. We are encouraged to have an active and living relationship with Him that doesn't stand on ceremony – a relationship that's not stuffy, but real. Many believers perceive God as 'Abba' or 'Father' in a healing, warm and relational way. But while this informality is what many appreciate about the Christian faith, we may be tempted to think about God the Father in an almost too-casual way that doesn't also acknowledge His supreme holiness and awesome power. If we read the verses above, we learn that Jesus intercedes with God the Father on our behalf. It's Jesus – and His sacrifice – that makes our relationship with God the Father possible.

Because God the Father is sovereign, we need to obey what He says, just as Jesus did. We read in Philippians 2:5-8:

> Your attitude should be the same as that of Christ Jesus:
>
> Who, being in very nature God,
> did not consider equality with God
> something to be grasped,
> but made himself nothing,
> taking the very nature of a servant,
> being made in human likeness,
> And being found in appearance as man,
> he humbled himself
> and became obedient to death –
> even death on a cross!

Now, chances are that part of 'your attitude being the same as that of Christ Jesus' won't involve actual death on a cross. Instead, the key message is to do with outlook: we are to 'make ourselves nothing', as Jesus did, and take on the very nature of a servant.

SERVANTHOOD

So, what does it mean to be a servant? What does the job description entail?

The *Oxford Dictionary* defines a servant as:

1. a person employed to do domestic work in a household or as a personal attendant;
2. an employee considered as performing services for his employer; and
3. a devoted follower, a person willing to serve another.

On the other hand, the *Oxford Dictionary* defines a slave thus:

1. a person who is owned by another and has to serve him;
2. a drudge, a person working very hard; and
3. a helpless victim of some dominating influence.

There's quite a distinction between these two definitions – servants are employed, while slaves are owned. This means servants receive wages. Romans 6:23 tells us,

> For the wages of sin is death, but the gift of God is eternal life in Christ Jesus our Lord.

Our Christian wages start with something priceless: salvation. But there are other benefits, too – such as provision, having God work in and through us, fellowship, and displaying the fruit of the Spirit in our lives as stated in Galatians 5:22:

> But the fruit of the Spirit is love, joy, peace, longsuffering, kindness, goodness, faithfulness, gentleness, self-control.

Servants can leave and choose another position if they wish to; slaves are forced to do the work assigned them. Servants are employed to work on behalf of their master for an acceptable wage; slaves must work for whatever the master deems as acceptable pay. It is the master who sets the agenda. The master directs the servant, and the servant responds. A Christ-like servant should demonstrate devotion and willingness – and the aim of that devotion and willingness is to serve others. A great example is found in the Book of Genesis. Eliezer of Damascus became patriarch Abraham's trusted servant, almost an administrative assistant, who helped his master with many important functions, including taking a long journey to find a bride for Abraham's son, Isaac. Eliezer's role represented a strong position of authority on behalf of Abraham. He obviously took his position seriously and conducted himself professionally and ethically, resulting in the successful marriage of Rebecca with Isaac. Eliezer proved himself a valuable supporter in other ways too, and that is why we remember him today, thousands of years later.

No matter how close a master-servant relationship is, a master does not need to give his servant an explanation of his plans and motivations. If a master says to a servant, 'I want you to take this parcel to the post office and send it,' a servant doesn't say, 'What's in the package? Why are you sending it? Are you sure about putting it in the mail? What about organising a courier pick-up instead?' The servant carries out the assigned duties without getting nosy about the process.

We have a mighty master whom we can trust to accomplish what needs to be done in the best way. Here are some verses that describe our God:

> Yours, O LORD, is the greatness and the power, and the glory and the majesty and the splendour, for everything in heaven and earth is yours. (1 Chronicles 29:11)

> Great is our Lord and mighty in power; his understanding has no limit. (Psalm 147:5)

> I am the Lord, the God of all mankind. Is anything too hard for me? (Jeremiah 32:27)

Remember, faith is about whether the object of our trust can perform according to the promise made. Our God is worth putting faith in and is worthy of our service.

Servanthood and hope

The idea of servanthood is vital to grasp if our Christian life is going to make sense. We need to understand that God is our master, not just our brother. One of the things that may undermine our feelings of faith and hope is when we feel personally disadvantaged by circumstances. However, sometimes it isn't about you. God may ask some difficult things of us, and may allow us to experience difficulties, because He wants to achieve good things in the lives of others. Sometimes He will let you know what those things are; sometimes He won't. God, as our master, does not have to explain – and it's not our right to know.

Jonah's story

Let's return to the story of Jonah and look at God's reaction to him wanting his own way. In Jonah 4:4 we read,

> But the Lord replied, 'Have you any right to be angry?'

Jonah has no verbal response to God's question. Instead, he takes himself away, builds a little shelter, and sits there feeling grumpy. God then grows a vine over the shelter to protect Jonah from the sun's heat while he gets over himself.

When Jonah sulks, God sends a worm to chew the vine. The protective foliage withers and dies. This makes Jonah even angrier, and he repeats his assertion:

> It would be better for me to die than to live. (Jonah 4:8)

God responds in this way:

> You have been concerned about this vine, though you did not tend it or make it grow. It sprang up overnight and died overnight. But Nineveh has more than a hundred and twenty thousand people who cannot tell their right hand from their left, and many cattle as well. Should I not be concerned about that great city?

I think God was quite gracious to Jonah, first, by providing Jonah with the vine as shelter while he sulked, and, second, in the way He spoke to Jonah. He gently tries to tell Jonah that He, God, has other priorities, that all people matter, and that He is sovereign. After all, God is the master, and Jonah the servant.

Who are we more like? Are we like Jesus who made himself nothing to die for the sins of the world? Or are we like Jonah, sitting under cover and sulking because God hasn't done what we expect Him to do? Which example do we want to follow?

FEAR OF SERVANTHOOD

Earlier we looked at some benefits of servanthood (provision, God's work in and through us, fellowship, the fruit of the Spirit), but one benefit not mentioned was the fact that an outward focus brings its own rewards. Helping someone else is one of the best feelings we can experience. At first thought, a servant's role does not sound very glorious. Who wants to use their time and resources to care for others? Wouldn't we rather invest our energies into having fun or serving our own interests?

But studies show that helping others in need promotes well-being for both giver and receiver. The immune system is stoked to perform more effectively, and stress is reduced to promote positivity and calm. It is true that it is more blessed to give than receive. As we give to others, God enriches us spiritually, expanding our hope and trust in His character to meet our personal needs. Serving others is actually a way of serving God. Whatever we do to help someone, Jesus said, it is serving Him.

We're going to talk more about this subject in the coming chapters, but here we need to realise this: servanthood isn't a bad trade-off for salvation. However, fear can lead to doubt. We can know that God is mighty. We can know that God is sovereign. We can know that God is worthy of faith. But, at the same time, we can also be afraid of what

God might ask us to do. Will He take away the things we cling to for security? Will He send us to the mission field where we'll never be heard from again? What will happen if we completely surrender to His will? Do we know what to expect or how we will feel?

Fear is the opposite of hope. It does not come from God. It makes the assumption that we will have to face things in our own strength and with limited resources. In fact, nothing could be further from the truth. God just wants us to be willing and available. Remember what we learned from 1 Thessalonians 5:24:

> The one who calls you is faithful and *he will do it*.

Not you; God.

And think about what Jesus says in John 15:5:

> I am the vine; you are the branches. If a man remains in me and I in him, he will bear much fruit; apart from me you can do nothing.

This is how Jesus lived.

He did not live by self-effort, but by the power of God. He was willing and available to do whatever God wanted. As Christians, our job is not to try and live like God without God (which is basically what Adam and Eve tried to do), but to let God live in and through us. If you embrace this realisation, much of the fear you may be feeling will fade away.

QUESTIONS FOR REFLECTION

Have you considered that some of the external things (e.g. events, insults, rejections, or grief) that have happened to you might have been part of serving God? What negative effects have you experienced?

_____
_____
_____
_____

How has your outlook about servanthood impacted your internal state in terms of your sense of hope?

_____
_____
_____
_____

In what ways have your past actions been those of a servant in God's kingdom?

_____
_____
_____
_____

Hope Rising

Do you feel you are currently making a deliberate choice to be a servant in God's kingdom? In what ways do you feel you need to make different choices?

_____
_____
_____
_____

In what ways do you think your current relationship with God is negatively impacted by your perspective on servanthood, including your fear of such an idea?

_____
_____
_____
_____

CHAPTER SIX

SIGNIFICANT SUFFERING

Suffering is not a popular topic, but, as with the material we've covered so far, it's an important experience to understand. We're going to look at suffering from two angles: its significance, and how to manage when it seems unbearable. We'll then consider how suffering fits within a framework of hope.

THE SIGNIFICANCE OF SUFFERING

In previous chapters we've considered three key ways in which our mindsets and understanding can affect feelings of hope: entitlement, asking why, and servanthood.

In terms of entitlement, we looked at how we can expect God's love, justice, guidance, and provision according to what He determines as our needs, rather than what we think we are owed or deserve. As the Bible tells us, God's ways are not our ways. He looks at our predicaments differently than we do.

We then looked at how the question of 'why?' is sometimes unhelpful. Getting off-focus can undermine our faith and impact our hope. While God endowed us with the tendency to be inquisitive and the desire to pursue understanding, there are limits to what we can humanly grasp and what we morally have a right to expect from God. Achieving the right balance between human concern and spiritual trust should be a paramount goal for Christians.

We've also looked at servanthood: God is the master and we are the servants. We are not entitled to question God – nor are we required to act independently of Him. He wants us to be willing and available – and *He will do it* according to His will and plan.

But even if you understand these ideas and acknowledge that what God gives you is worth more than what He wants from you, there may still be a feeling that this equation shouldn't include suffering. Why would God want us to suffer? What can be gained from our pain? Surely the God of love wouldn't allow us to struggle and experience deprivation as a means of demonstrating His love?

The following reminders may help us to better understand God:

1. **God wants the best for us:** Romans 8:28 says,

   > And we know that in all things God works for the good of those who love him, who have been called according to his purpose.

   This is good news indeed. But don't forget, our mindsets come into play here. Our definition of *good* may differ from God's.

2. **We live in an imperfect world:** As explored in the last chapter, when humans walked away from an intimate relationship with God, a chain of events unfolded that

differed from God's loving design. The consequence is that the choices of others have caused significant suffering in this world throughout history. Like it or not, we are part of this chain of events. We shouldn't expect perfection in this life, but rather in the next, where

> He will wipe every tear from their eyes. There will be no more death or mourning or crying or pain, for the old order of things (will pass) away. (Revelation 21:4)

3. **Our actions have an impact:** It is easy to sit back and blame God for leading us into suffering, but we need to be honest about our circumstances. Sometimes we get ourselves into trouble through personal actions, inactions, or choices. We must take responsibility for our role in any situation. We struggle to face our weaknesses and accept criticism. But we must be who we are and honestly assess our role in every outcome.

4. **Suffering is to be expected:** We learn in 1 Peter 4:12,

> ...do not be surprised at the painful trial you are suffering, as though something strange were happening to you.

Paul also explains to the Thessalonians that suffering is part of life when he says,

> We sent Timothy, who is our brother and God's fellow worker in spreading the gospel of Christ, to

> strengthen and encourage you in your faith, so that no one would be unsettled by these trials. You know quite well that we were destined for them. (1 Thessalonians 3:2-3)

So, how do we reconcile the fact that God wants the best for us, but suffering is to be expected? Here are some points of view that may be helpful:

SUFFERING LEADS TO GOOD THINGS
In Romans 5:3-4 Paul explains,

> We also rejoice in our sufferings, because we know that suffering produces perseverance; perseverance, character; and character, hope.

That's quite a list. We inevitably suffer in many instances of our lives, which if conducted in a Godly manner, leads to perseverance. Perseverance builds character, and character clings to hope. Hope is just what we're looking for. But, interestingly, hope isn't at the beginning of the list; it's at the end. We don't use hope to escape suffering. Hope comes from working our way through suffering.

SUFFERING PREPARES US FOR THE FUTURE
In 2 Corinthians 4:16-17 we read:

> Therefore, we do not lose heart. Though outwardly we are wasting away, yet inwardly we are being renewed day by day. For our light and momentary troubles are

achieving for us an eternal glory that far outweighs them all.

Meanwhile, Acts 14:22 tells us:

> We must go through many hardships to enter the kingdom of God.

There is a similar pattern in the natural world. You'd think that wind would be the enemy of trees – and, indeed, strong wind sometimes causes trees to fall. But scientists have discovered that when trees are grown in a biodome, these plants often grow to a certain height, then collapse. Because a biodome has no wind, scientists have come to the surprising conclusion that wind actually strengthens a plant. The effects of the wind enable trees to stand strong as they grow taller. It is the same with us. Suffering strengthens us for the future.

SUFFERING CAUSES COURSE CORRECTIONS

As mentioned above, we sometimes suffer because of the choices we've made. Other times, God allows us to go through a time of suffering as a way of bringing us back on track.

Hebrews 12:5-6 says:

> And have you completely forgotten this word of encouragement that addresses you as a father addresses his son? It says,

> 'My son, do not make light of the Lord's discipline,
> and do not lose heart when he rebukes you,
> because the Lord disciplines those he loves,
> and he punishes everyone he accepts as a son.'

As children growing up, we often struggle with the concept of rules. We want to set our own course and make our own decisions, to have our own way. Yet, we're not mature enough to realise that some of those decisions will have serious consequences, that rules are usually meant to keep us safe and teach us how to be decent and caring human beings. And, of course, when we did misbehave, most of us loathed the times when we underwent disciplinary measures as a result of our failure to stick to the rules.

But, as many parents will agree, a corresponding lack of rules and discipline can have serious consequences. Children need boundaries. Without them, life can fall apart in tragic ways. As Christians, boundaries help rather than hinder; they protect us from within our faith.

Listen to these words from Proverbs:

> My son, keep to your father's commands and do not forsake your mother's teaching. For these commands are a lamp, this teaching is a light, and the corrections of discipline are the way to life. (6:20,23)

and

> He who ignores discipline despises himself, but whoever heeds correction gains understanding. (15:32)

SUFFERING TESTS

There is a link between suffering and the testing of faith. In 1 Peter 1:6-7 we read:

> ...though now for a little while you may have had to suffer grief in all kinds of trials. These have come so that your faith – of greater worth than gold, which perishes even though refined by fire – may be proved genuine and may result in praise, glory, and honour when Jesus Christ is revealed.

James 1:2-3 tells us:

> Consider it pure joy, my brothers, whenever you face trials of many kinds, because you know that the testing of your faith develops perseverance.

Meanwhile, Jesus tells us,

> I am the vine; you are the branches. If a man remains in me and I in him, he will bear much fruit; apart from me you can do nothing. (John 15:5)

We learn key lessons in these three passages of Scripture. First, suffering tests our faith, and, like the refiner's fire, burns away the dross from our lives. Second, we should consider trials to be so much of a good thing that we view them a joy. This is more difficult – usually on account of the suffering we're enduring. Adopting such thinking is another way we are transformed by the renewing of our minds.

Third, Jesus reminds us that we are to remain in Him, and that apart from Him we can do nothing. The trouble is that when trials strike, we often struggle to remain connected. We sometimes distance ourselves from God or find it difficult to pray. Our faith is tested, and hope crumbles. If this scenario resonates with you, take some time to re-examine your mindset: your feelings of entitlement, whether you are questioning God about why this is happening to you, and your attitude as a servant. Remind yourself of the purpose of suffering. Look for possible positive outcomes that might evolve. For example, if you are a single parent who cannot find employment, maybe your child needs extra time and attention from you right now. When the need is successfully met, God will provide a job.

Suffering leads to dependence on God

Following on from the teachings of Jesus about remaining in Him is the idea that suffering can and should push us closer to God, not further away. When we are seeking to live by faith, suffering causes us to ask for God's strength and intervention because we know we can't do anything without Him. The outcome is a deeper relationship with Him and acceptance of our circumstances.

We read in 1 Peter 4:19,

> So then, those who suffer according to God's will should commit themselves to their faithful Creator and continue to do good.

JESUS' STORY
Let's go back to Philippians 2:5-8:

> In your relationship with one another, have the same mindset as Christ Jesus:
>
> Who, being in very nature God,
> did not consider equality with God
> something to be grasped,
> but made himself nothing,
> taking the very nature of a servant,
> being made in human likeness,
> And being found in appearance as man,
> he humbled himself
> and became obedient to death –
> even death on a cross!

Don't forget that Jesus is the Son of God. Think about what He gave up in order to come to us as our Saviour. He made himself nothing. Everything He did while on earth He did by relying on His Father. That's why He was without sin: total obedience and reliance on God.

When thinking about your own life, strive for dependence on God. Let God work in, and through, you. Realise that God made you in His image, He has a plan for your life, and He will help you to accomplish it.

Suffering for your Faith
2 Timothy 3:12 says,

> In fact, everyone who wants to live a godly life in Christ Jesus will be persecuted.

The Apostle Paul knew what he was talking about when he spoke of persecution. Prior to his conversion, he had been a master persecutor, and was subsequently required to suffer for his Christian faith. Most of us are unlikely to face the same level of suffering as Paul, but there are times when the truth that we hold to, standing up for what's right, and the decisions we make for God will lead us to places of discomfort. Such discomfort is a hallmark of following Jesus.

When Suffering Seems Too Much
We've now had a look at the significance of suffering – what suffering is for and what it can produce. Now we're going to take a look at times when the suffering we're enduring seems overwhelming.

Sometimes we use the phrase, 'It could be worse' to try to remind ourselves that while we are having a hard time, there are more serious outcomes that could happen. Other times, though, it's hard to imagine how things could get worse. Such times often involve significant loss. Fires or earthquakes can destroy homes or possessions. A tsunami can wipe out entire coastal communities. Accidents claim lives. People fall sick, become incapacitated, or die. Sometimes these things happen to us or the ones we love.

We can also grieve lost opportunities, broken marriages, infertility, and the restrictions that special needs or illnesses may mean for our lives. Loss is the most difficult situation. Grief is a heavy burden. Where loss is unexpected, we also have to deal with shock as well as grief. We struggle to process what has happened. We tell ourselves that the event surely couldn't be true. We strive to make sense of it by seeking answers or requesting justice or taking revenge – or by wanting to be left alone. And most of us will question God at some point through this process.

So how should we respond to devastating losses? In reality, each of us will deal with tragedy in a different way. There is no *right* way. However, here are a few general points that may help:

1. **It's okay to be sad:** Loving means attachment. Whenever we lose the object of attachment, there will be grief. That's okay. God's not asking you to feel nothing. What's less okay is when sadness overwhelms you to the point that you become unreachable – either by God or by others. Strive to stay connected even in your sadness. There may be times when you feel the need to be alone. That's fine. Just don't let that urge dominate your life. We are designed to be people who build relationships with others in families, school, jobs, communities, and church. Alone, we lose confidence and struggle with limited ability. Together, we grow stronger and more competent.

2. **Take time to process:** 'Time heals all wounds' has become a cliché but there is truth in the saying. Time does make a difference. What you've experienced could prove to be something you never get over, but you can get through it. Whatever the situation, allow yourself

time to grieve your loss. How much time it takes to get through the heartache will vary from person to person and probably reflect the significance of your pain. Find ways to process what has happened, whether through journaling, counselling, or taking time to think and pray – or all three.

3. **Consider your mindset:** Think about the points we've already covered. Are you blaming God for things caused by the actions of others? Do you feel you shouldn't have to experience loss? Are you asking why God has put you through such an ordeal? Are you allowing your tragedy to erode your faith and undermine feelings of hope? Have you harboured unrealistic expectations about the fact that everything, including people, comes to an end?

4. **Don't suffer in silence:** Keep talking about how you are feeling. Get it out rather than hiding your emotions. Seek professional help from counsellors or pastors if you need it, and begin to learn the skills to manage and process grief. Ask friends and church members to pray for you. Let other people into your life, for as it says in Galatians 6:2,

> Carry each other's burdens and, in this way, you will fulfil the law of Christ.

Sometimes, this may involve putting aside feelings of self-pity or pride.

5. **Be prepared to let go:** At some point, you need to turn a corner. We discussed earlier the fact that hope looks forward. Eventually, you need to get to the point where you start to look toward, and plan for whatever comes next. This involves letting go of what has happened in the past. It will take time – and God is a God of compassion – He doesn't expect this process to happen overnight. What's not so good is when a person is unable to ever let go of a tragic loss or prolonged grief. Life is ultimately about living – and as a servant of the Lord, He will have work for you to do.

6. **Accept help:** Some people find this much easier than others. Accepting help is often difficult for a number of reasons. One barrier may be that you don't want to talk about your problems with just anyone. What you're going through may be hard to discuss, or your feelings may be difficult to put into words. But help doesn't have to involve talking. Let people offer practical support – meals or finances or respite or housecleaning – whatever is needed. You don't have to let everyone in. And there's nothing wrong in being honest and saying that while you appreciate help, you just can't talk about your pain at this time. Don't let pride or fear get in the way of accepting assistance from others. Help is, after all, a form of hope.

7. **Stay connected:** We've already covered this in the first bullet point, but it's worth reiterating. Stay connected to people, but, more importantly, stay connected to God.

> Faith is not a feeling; faith is a choice. Choose to stay connected to God in whatever ways you can.

SUFFERING AND HOPE

Toward the beginning of this chapter we looked at Romans 5:3-4 where Paul explains,

> We also rejoice in our sufferings, because we know that suffering produces perseverance; perseverance, character; and character, hope.

We saw earlier that hope comes at the end, not the beginning of this amazing list, but it's worth questioning why this might be. Surely hope is what we need in order to get through suffering rather than serve as a by-product of trials and tribulations? Perhaps the answer to this conundrum lies in the verse from Romans that we looked at in Chapter Two:

> Do not conform any longer to the pattern of this world, but be transformed by the renewing of your mind. (Romans 12:2a)

As we suffer and persevere, we learn important things about God and about ourselves. Our character matures, and we start to understand life not from our own perspective, but from an eternal point of view. We become transformed by the renewing of our minds.

> Then you will be able to test and approve what God's will is – his good, pleasing and perfect will. (Romans 12:2)

Because, when all is said and done, God's will and the blessings He has in store for us are of supreme value. As it says in 1 Peter 4:13,

> But rejoice that you participate in the sufferings of Christ, so that you may be overjoyed when his glory is revealed.

This is kingdom thinking, not human thinking – a true transforming of the mind.

ONE FINAL THOUGHT

Suffering also brings another consequence: it enables us to better understand the plight of others and to reach out to help them. 2 Corinthians 1:3-5 says,

> Praise be to the God and Father of our Lord Jesus Christ, the Father of compassion and the God of all comfort, who comforts us in all our troubles, so that we can comfort those in any trouble with the comfort we ourselves have received from God. For just as the sufferings of Christ flow over into our lives, so also through Christ comfort overflows.

We live in an imperfect world full of hurting people. Don't let your own feelings of sorrow or self-pity stand between you and helping others. In doing so, you will take a big step forward in your own recovery. We'll look at this in more detail later.

QUESTIONS FOR REFLECTION

How have you dealt with the external things (e.g. events, insults, rejections, or grief) that have happened to you? Can you say you have rejoiced in your suffering, or have you blamed God for bringing it to your door?

_____
_____
_____

How has your outlook about suffering impacted your internal state in terms of hope?

_____
_____
_____

In what ways have your past actions indicated a lack of understanding about the role of suffering in our faith journey?

_____
_____
_____

Significant Suffering

How will a new understanding of the role that suffering plays in our faith journey influence your choices now?

_____
_____
_____
_____

In what way is your current relationship with God negatively impacted by your perspective on suffering, including your fears?

_____
_____
_____
_____

CHAPTER SEVEN

GLORIOUS GRATITUDE

Let's start this chapter with a quick recap of where we've been so far. We've looked at:

- What hope is and why it's important.
- The role of mindset in our lives and the way in which our attitude and outlook plays a big part in how we feel and think about personal circumstances.
- How entitlement affects our expectations.
- Why asking 'why?' can be unhelpful.
- Enhanced awareness that God is master and we are His servants.
- What we might surprisingly gain from suffering.
- How to manage significant suffering.

The purpose of focusing on these aspects of our lives is to take an honest look at our thought processes to determine whether how we think and how we perceive God supports or undermines our feelings of hope. Perhaps, through this process, you've been able to better understand yourself – and God – and can begin to come to terms with your circumstances. As we clarify and commit to a relationship with God, many areas of life will improve as a result, including our perspective on hope.

Let's now take a step further by looking at the subject of gratitude – because it's one thing to be able to say, 'Okay, I accept this aspect of my life as part of being a Christian' but it is another to then feel grateful.

Gratitude is a key element of being able to experience hope.

The *Oxford Dictionary* defines gratitude as follows:

> Being thankful, feeling or showing that one values a kindness or benefit received.

That's pretty basic – someone does something for us that is kind or beneficial and we express thanks. But what happens when what we experience doesn't feel kind or doesn't seem to benefit us; what then? Are we supposed to feel grateful for difficulties?

In the last chapter we examined the significance of suffering – that it's not for nothing. As part of this we looked at 1 Peter 1:6-7:

> ...though now for a little while you may have had to suffer grief in all kinds of trials. These have come so that your faith – of greater worth than gold, which perishes even though refined by fire – may be proved genuine and may result in praise, glory and honour when Jesus Christ is revealed.

Through this Scripture we come to understand that trials

do ultimately benefit us. But can we actually be grateful for them? Surely not. Yet in 1 Thessalonians 5:16-18 Paul says:

> Be joyful always; pray continually; give thanks in all circumstances.

PAUL'S STORY

The Apostle Paul began public life by persecuting Christians, until God called him to put aside his old ways and live a new kind of life. He changed sides and became a preacher, teacher, evangelist, and writer of key letters found in the New Testament from which we can learn about living as an active Christian. He was also an accidental tourist, taking long missionary journeys across parts of Asia and Europe to encourage believers and spread the Good News.

His life was filled with trials: imprisonment, persecution, flogging, shipwreck. He fell out with one of his colleagues (see Acts 15:36-40) and didn't always get on with the disciples, either. He worked as a tent maker. We know he had poor eyesight and, after boasting about how much he had suffered for Christ (2 Corinthians 11:16-33), he then confessed that something tormented him:

> To keep me from becoming conceited because of these surpassingly great revelations, there was given me a thorn in my flesh. (2 Corinthians 12:7)

We aren't told what this thorn is, but we come to see that Paul wasn't perfect even if he was passionate and committed to God.

Indeed, Paul was someone whose passion for serving the Lord – and his understanding of his role in God's kingdom – meant that he was no stranger to suffering. In the end, he lost his life for his faith. It's interesting, then, to read what he says about his feelings toward this suffering when he writes to the Philippians:

> I rejoice greatly in the Lord that at last you have renewed your concern for me. Indeed, you have been concerned, but you had no opportunity to show it. I am not saying this because I am in need, for I have learned to be content whatever the circumstances. I know what it is to be in need, and I know what it is to have plenty. I have learned the secret of being content in any and every situation, whether well fed or hungry, whether living in plenty or in want. I can do everything through him who gives me strength. (Philippians 4:10-13)

There are probably not many of us who could 'boast' quite as much as Paul about what we've had to endure. But if he could endure and talk about being thankful and content, then we would do well to try to understand how he could say such things – and mean them.

CONNECTION IS KEY

Here are some lessons we learn from Paul in 1 Thessalonians 5:16-18 as mentioned above:

Paul talks about being joyful always. From a Christian perspective, what we need to understand is that *joy* and *happiness* are not the same thing. Joy is listed as a fruit of the Spirit (Galatians 5:22-23), and the *fruit* of the Spirit are just that – a natural product of the Spirit who dwells within us. We aren't supposed to bring forth quality fruit on our own. These qualities come from allowing God to work in and through us. The only way that can happen is to build a meaningful relationship with Him and nurture it on a daily basis.

In terms of gratitude, we can, and should be grateful for our relationship with God, for our salvation, and for the indwelling of the Holy Spirit. Making and maintaining that connection with God is key – and being grateful makes the connection easier. How can we not be thankful? God created us and the world around us. He provides for our needs. He sent His only Son – Jesus – to show us how to live and to pay for our sins.

PRAYER IS VITAL

The Apostle Paul talks about praying continually. This probably sounds like an impossibility. Many of us would probably be lucky to manage five minutes a day, much less praying frequently or continually. Our circumstances sometimes make it difficult to pray. We may not be able to find the words. Some find it hard to pray when all is well, but turn to God when things get tough. Others are the exact opposite – they can pray when things are fine, but fall silent in times of trouble.

However, it is possible to live in an *attitude* of prayer without always speaking words.

Paul teaches in Romans 8:26-27:

> In the same way, the Spirit helps us in our weakness. We do not know what we ought to pray for, but the Spirit himself intercedes for us with groans that words cannot express. And he who searches our hearts, knows the mind of the Spirit, because the Spirit intercedes for the saints in accordance with God's will.

How great is that? We don't have to know the words to get it right. In fact, prayer is not a magic formula that some people have mastered and others haven't. An attitude of prayer is one of understanding and connection – of placing ourselves in the Master's hands and relying on Him. This is another gift for which we can be extremely grateful.

'IN' – NOT 'FOR'

This may seem like a small distinction, but the verse clearly says to 'give thanks *in* all circumstances.' It doesn't say to give thanks *for* all circumstances. This means that God is not expecting you to be grateful for having lost someone, or for an illness you might be enduring, or because someone has broken your heart or offended you. It would be extremely challenging for us to express such thanks and still be honest.

However, if you appreciate how things work together

(essentially, the list of things mentioned in the recap at the beginning of this chapter), you can be grateful that, for whatever reason (and you don't have to know the reason), God is with you and will help you get through whatever has come your way.

Here are some things we can learn from Paul in Philippians 4:10-13, as mentioned above:

CONTENTMENT IS KEY

Paul states in this passage, 'I have learned the secret of being content in any and every situation, whether well fed or hungry, whether living in plenty or in want.' This is impressive. To be content in any situation? The good and the bad? It sounds not only impressive, but nearly impossible.

Yet, when you think about it, can you imagine a scenario in which contentment wouldn't make things better? Where being able to be still, calm, and at peace is a natural state? It certainly sounds like an attractive way to live.

Humans have always struggled with contentment. In fact, if Adam and Eve had been content – not wanting more – history might have turned out very differently. Yet, God knows we struggle with the need to be content. One of the Ten Commandments states:

> You shall not covet your neighbour's house. You shall not covet your neighbour's wife, or his manservant or maidservant, his ox or donkey, or anything that belongs to your neighbour. (Exodus 10:17)

Coveting – or wanting what you haven't got – is the opposite of contentment. But these days, contentment is rare in our consumer society, where there is always something bigger, better, stronger, greater for us to get or buy so that we can be happy. Add to this our basic survival instinct, feelings of ambition, and mindsets oriented to entitlement, it's amazing anyone is content at all. We never seem to have enough, and thus, we seldom feel gratitude and fail to express thanks to God for all He has given us.

Contentment is worth pursuing, and contentment and gratitude go hand in hand. Thankfulness is good for both body and soul, reducing stress, enhancing joy, and making us mindful of all the ways our lives are enriched by a grateful heart toward God.

So, where do we start? In 1 Thessalonians 4:11 Paul says,

> Make it your ambition to lead a quiet life, to mind your own business and to work with your hands just as we told you.

Perhaps a desire for contentment begins with living quietly and working faithfully where God has placed you.

PRACTICE IS REQUIRED

It's clear, though, from Philippians 4:12 that contentment doesn't happen overnight. When Paul says, 'I have learned the secret', this doesn't mean that he found a special code in a book or fortune cookie, or in a cave full of treasure. It means he learned the secret through practice. He doesn't expand on this or say how long it took him to master the art of contentment, but master it he did, setting an example through his ministry that each of us can choose to follow if we want to become more Christ-like.

Part of this process likely involved changing his mindset. We'll look into this more in the next chapter. For now, be aware that contentment won't necessarily happen overnight, but, with practice, it can eventually blossom so that we reap a harvest of gratitude.

CONTENTMENT IS LINKED TO CONNECTION

Perhaps the most important part of Philippians 4:10-13 appears in the last verse, which says,

> I can do everything through him who gives me strength.

Here, Paul clearly states that everything he does is God-powered. And while it's likely that some of his ability to be content came from his thinking (being transformed by the renewing of his mind), a big part came from the fact that he lived his life as a willing and available servant of God.

This process starts with being born again (see John 3:3-7) and involves what is sometimes referred to as 'dying to self'. Paul talks about this in Romans 6:4-8:

> We were therefore buried with him through baptism into death in order that, just as Christ was raised from the dead through the glory of the Father, we too may live a new life.

> If we have been united with him like this in death, we will certainly also be united with him in his resurrection. For we know that our old self was crucified with him so that the body of sin might be done away with, that we should no longer be slaves to sin – because anyone who has died has

been freed from sin. Now if we died with Christ, we believe that we will also live with him.

Christianity is about connectedness. Our faith requires us to be willing to die to self and put how we used to think or act behind us. We must allow God to live in and through us. Being a Christian means being God-powered, not self-powered. And this is something we have to choose on a daily basis until, like Paul, we master the art of dying to self and begin to settle into a state of contentment.

In addition, here are other things we should know about committing to a life of gratitude, contentment, and connectedness:

PRACTICE TAKES PRESENCE

At the beginning of this book we looked at the definition of hope as the expectation and desire for a certain event to occur. We observed the fact that hope looks toward a future event or outcome. But gratitude works in a slightly different way. Gratitude is about *now* – about this current moment – about stopping and noticing and giving thanks for what is happening in your life at *this very minute*.

Earlier in the book we saw that, even though there are times to look back and assess where we've come from, it is unhelpful to be always look back. In the same way, though hope has a future perspective, we can become so focused on the future, especially if we want to change our present circumstances, that we forget to live now. In truth, however, we only have now. The past is gone, and who knows what lies ahead or how our situation may change tomorrow or next week or next month or next year? Jesus reminded us to focus on one day a time.

What opportunities could we be missing by not living now, but rather, focusing on the past or future?

How might a future-focus be affecting our mindset, our feelings of entitlement, and our expectations?

Is thinking or worrying about the future stopping us from feeling grateful, contented, and connected now?

In order to learn the secret of contentment, as Paul did, we need to focus on what's before us in this moment rather than on what's ahead of us tomorrow and thereafter. Of course, it makes sense to plan ahead and be prepared. But obsessing about the future without adequate attention to the present and living now is often counter-productive.

COMPARISON CAN BE DANGEROUS
Earlier in the chapter we looked at Exodus 10:17:

> You shall not covet your neighbour's house. You shall not covet your neighbour's wife, or his manservant or maidservant, his ox or donkey, or anything that belongs to your neighbour.

We have looked at the fact that being content these days is difficult because of the consumer society in which we live. But if you think about it, this 'coveting' often starts with comparisons. If you look at your neighbour's house, or marriage, or lifestyle, or possessions and compare these with what you have, you may want more and feel like you're missing out. In fact, you might not just want more, you might feel you're entitled to more, and we've already looked at the risks of entitlement.

In making comparisons, you may also start to make

Hope Rising

value judgments about what the other person should or should not have. You might feel as though he or she doesn't deserve what they have, or even that it's unfair that their life is so perfect while you suffer beneath the weight of untold burdens. Yet, in Matthew 7:1-2, Jesus says:

> Do not judge, or you too will be judged. For in the same way you judge others, you will be judged, and with the measure you use, it will be measured to you.

Gulp. That doesn't sound good, does it?

Besides, while a person may look happy and healthy and prosperous on the outside, only God knows the truth. Someone may be dealing with all sorts of problems or difficulties that you have no idea about – issues that most people don't broadcast to the general public. The image portrayed on Facebook is unlikely to be the full reality. And, ultimately, when it comes to possessions, two things are true: material belongings don't make you happy and, whatever you own, when it comes to the end of your life, you can't take it with you. Remember the words of Jesus, which He spoke just before the passage about not judging others, in Matthew 6:19-21:

> Do not store up for yourselves treasure on earth, where moth and rust destroy, and where thieves break in and steal. But store up for yourselves treasures in heaven, where moth and rust do not destroy, and where thieves do not break in and steal. For where your treasure is, there your heart will be also.

Only you can say where your heart is right now – longing after the things of this earth or keeping in mind the life to come.

GRATITUDE, CONNECTEDNESS AND HOPE

Remember that gratitude, thankfulness, and contentment come from connectedness. The more we 'learn the secret' of being connected to God, the more grateful we are going to be. And, as we become more connected to God and more content with now, something interesting happens: our hope begins to flourish into eternal trust and faith, as reflected in Hebrews 10:23 (emphasis added):

> Let us hold unswervingly to the hope we profess, *for he who promised is faithful.*

It's hard to be hopeful if you're always feeling short-changed. Being grateful is a choice we need to make each day. In summary, gratitude involves the following:

- A healthy perspective on your life – including your mindset and attitude.
- Not spending time comparing what you don't have with what others possess.
- Holding realistic expectations.
- A deep appreciation for what God is doing in your life.
- Being prepared to use what God has given you to help others (more about that later).

Start practising gratitude today, actively thanking God for the blessings that have filled your life.

Hope Rising

Make a list of all the blessings you receive in one day's time: health, home, income, transportation, family, friends, and a long list of possessions. Then praise God for them, asking for an attitude of appreciation as well as the wisdom to use your countless resources for His glory.

QUESTIONS FOR REFLECTION

In what ways are you grateful in all circumstances as you have dealt with external things (e.g. events, insults, rejections, or grief) that have happened to you?

_____
_____
_____

How has your outlook about gratitude and contentment impacted your internal state in terms of hope?

_____
_____
_____
_____

How far into the process of 'learning the secret' of contentment do you think you are? Do you see a link between a lack of contentment, a lack of gratitude, and a lack of connectedness?

_____
_____
_____
_____

Hope Rising

What choices have you made that have made things worse for you because of your lack of understanding about the roles of gratitude, contentment, and connectedness?

_____

_____

_____

_____

In what way would living in the present rather than focusing on the future positively impact your current relationship with God? Do you rely on God to give you the strength to live today?

_____

_____

_____

_____

CHAPTER EIGHT

Re-examining and Reframing

It's time to pull the threads of our thinking together. We need to see where we're at in terms of being transformed by the renewing of our minds – and, as a consequence, where our feelings of hope now sit.

To help with this process, consider the five key aspects of hope that we explored in Chapter One: the external, the internal, our actions, our choices, and our relationship with God.

Answer the following questions with as much honesty as you can. And, as you do so, look back at some of your responses to the questions we've covered so far:

External influences

In what way do you feel as though you are beginning to gain a new perspective on the external things that have happened to you that have made you lose hope?

_____
_____
_____
_____

Have you been blaming God for the choices of others? Has your understanding of the way in which the world works, as opposed to what God originally had in mind for us, begun to change?

_____
_____
_____
_____

Have you begun to come to terms with leaving justice to God – that we must forgive others as we have been forgiven – and that we can rely on God to help us do that?

_____
_____
_____
_____

Do you feel as though you spend more time judging others rather than yourself, or comparing what you have with what others have? If so, how can you change this outlook?

_____
_____
_____
_____

Internal Thought Processes

How have your ideas about God and hope begun to change because of a new understanding of how your mindset has influenced your outlook?

_____
_____
_____
_____

Would you say you are looking forward or back? And do you remember to live now?

_____
_____
_____
_____

What do you still feel entitled to get out of this life? Is this more than what God promises?

_____
_____
_____
_____

Hope Rising

Would you say your expectations of God, and of life, are realistic or unrealistic? How do they fit in with what we learn about the Christian life from the Bible?

_____

_____

_____

_____

How is your attitude toward God beginning to change in regard to your understanding of suffering and gratitude?

_____

_____

_____

ACTION

If you've suffered in silence in the past or not allowed others to help you, what actions could you take to reach out and ask for help now?

_____

_____

_____

_____

What actions should you take to come to terms with what you've suffered? Do you need to let go or accept your sit-

Re-examining and Reframing

uation? Do you need professional help in order to take positive steps forward?

_____
_____
_____
_____

How connected are you to God? What actions should you take to become more connected with Him on a daily basis?

_____
_____
_____
_____

Choice

How has your thinking about God as our master begun to change? Do you feel as though you have a better understanding of His sovereignty? If so, in what way?

_____
_____
_____
_____

Have you previously known what it means to be a servant of God? Is being a servant of God (rather than just being a recipient of salvation) a role you have deliberately chosen?

Is this something you feel more prepared to choose now?
_____
_____
_____

In terms of embracing living now rather than always thinking about the future, what choices will help you to be more present in your current life?
_____
_____
_____

What choices are you making to 'store up treasures in heaven'?
_____
_____
_____

Your relationship with God

What is your overall attitude toward God? Do you feel as though you have begun to change your view of Christian faith through understanding the doctrine from an eternal perspective? In what way are you beginning to have a dif-

Re-examining and Reframing

ferent outlook about how God might use suffering in order to prepare you for Kingdom work?

_____
_____
_____
_____

If you have a fear of serving, where does this come from? Do you need to practise more at letting God work in and through you? What stops you from doing this?

_____
_____
_____
_____

Can you say, as Paul did, '*I can do everything through him who gives me strength*'? What could you do to make this truer for you?

_____
_____
_____
_____

That's a lot of questions! It's important to take some time to examine and re-examine your thinking – your mindset, your feelings of entitlement, and your expectations – until they better align with God's thinking. If some of these ideas are new to you, really understanding and adopting them may take time. That's okay. God is gracious, kind, and loving. What's important is to take a step forward, to head in the right direction.

Don't forget that loss of hope can be a key indicator that your thinking and God's may not be aligned. If necessary, keep referring back to this material. Remind yourself and re-examine yourself as often as needed.

If you can better understand why you feel limited hope, you'll be in a better position to fix your thinking, take action, or make better choices. Is it because of a persistent mindset? Is it because you need reminders about the nature of being a servant? Are you harbouring feelings of unforgiveness toward someone who has wronged you? Do you need external help to address a difficult situation?

If you have spent years thinking in a certain way, it's going to take time to reframe your perspective. But it can be done. Despite our Christian beliefs, sometimes we seem to adopt default settings for our thought processes. If we go back to Fiona's story near the beginning of this book, her default setting was to catastrophise. As soon as anything unexpected happened, she would immediately think the worst. Fiona, through using the technique described in Chapter One, reframed her thinking by giving herself alternative thoughts.

At first, she found this process difficult. Then, when she realised how often she thought catastrophically, she felt panicky about that, too – she catastrophised about her catastrophic thinking. But within a short time, she stopped needing to rush to her journal to reframe her thinking.

Soon she was able to work through the process mentally to calm herself. Not long after that, her catastrophic thinking diminished almost completely.

Try to adopt a technique similar to that shown in Chapter One to help alter the mindset that caused you to lose hope. Remind yourself of the Kingdom perspective. Remember God's sovereignty and His trustworthiness. Remind yourself to rely on Him. And keep reminding yourself until, like Fiona, the changes become more permanent.

A focus on trusting and relying on God, maintaining a Kingdom perspective, and adopting techniques to change unhealthy thinking will help you re-examine and reframe your thinking – and put your feelings of hopelessness into proper perspective. We've already touched on some of these key areas, but let's look at them a little more closely.

TRUST

Trust is a two-way street. First, we need to trust God. This starts with belief, which then turns into faith. Faith results in salvation as we trust the object of our faith (God) to be able to deliver what He promises.

At this point we could fill pages with verse after verse about God's trustworthiness. However, if you identify a lack of trust in God as one of your sticking points, make it your aim to get to know God better. He is more than worthy of your faith and trust. With each day that dawns, every breath we take, and all of the situations we face, God is watching over us and guiding our actions through prayer, the Bible, and circumstances when we allow Him to.

But, not only do we need to trust God, we also need to be trustworthy ourselves. Paul says, in 1 Corinthians 4:2:

> Now it is required that those who have been given a trust must prove faithful.

Jesus also talks about being trustworthy in a number of parables:

- The Shrewd Manager (Luke 16:1-15)
- The Tenants (Matthew 21:33-44)
- The Faithful and Wise Servant (Matthew 24:45-51)
- The Ten Minas (Luke 19:11-27)
- The Watchful Servants (Mark 13:34-37)
- The Unfruitful Fig Tree (Luke 13:6-7)

Where do you stand in terms of trustworthiness? Can God trust you? Your answer will reveal much about your relationship with the Lord.

Adopt a Kingdom perspective

We may need a reminder that, like Jonah, it's not all about us. God will be patient as we learn this lesson – and He may well have grown you a metaphorical vine while you get there – but, ultimately, we have to come to the point where we understand that to be Christian is to be an instrument of God. Yes, we have freedom to make choices, but each one should be God-honouring and bring us closer to God, not pull us away.

In 1 Peter 2:4-5 our role is described like this:

> As you come to him, the living Stone – rejected by men but chosen by God and precious to him – you also, like living stones, are being built into a spiritual

Re-examining and Reframing

> house to be a holy priesthood, offering spiritual sacrifices acceptable to God through Jesus Christ.

And:

> But you are a chosen people, a royal priesthood, a holy nation, a people belonging to God, that you may declare the praises of him who called you out of darkness into his wonderful light. (verse 9)

As you read these verses, what springs to mind? Does this sound like the way you live? Have you adopted a Kingdom perspective? Do you 'declare the praises of him who called you?'

RELY ON GOD

Sometimes we lose hope because we feel afraid. Sometimes fear causes us to doubt whether we are able to accomplish a task or meet a goal. Sometimes we don't act because we don't think we are good enough. Yet, as mentioned several times over the course of this book, most of the time, all we need is to be willing and available – and let God do the rest. The Bible is full of many individuals who were not particularly skilled. Some had shady reputations. But they appear in the Bible as examples that reflect us. We all fall short, but we long for a close relationship with God. Making ourselves available and maintaining a focus on our Creator and the Kingdom are the two chief elements that God uses to shape our Christian character and further the Kingdom.

The Christian life is not about trying to pretend to be more like Christ; it's about becoming more Christ-like.

Don't try to be someone other than who God made you to be. You were born to be you, and as God works in your life, as you become more Christ-like, you will become the truest version of yourself. As humans, each of us is flawed, but God designed us with potential. He is perfecting us through faith, love, and hope. The best versions of ourselves are yet to come!

At this time, you might not necessarily be *where* you're supposed to be or *doing* what God intends for you to do, but never doubt that you *are* who God created – someone special and original and uniquely suited to the role God would have you fulfil.

So, just be you – but be the you who chooses to make yourself available to God. And, if you don't know who you are – or if the things that have happened to you over the course of your life have taken you far away from who that is – start at the beginning. Get to know yourself again – and get to know God.

LAURA'S STORY

Laura, like Fiona, grew up in a non-Christian home and suffered with low self-esteem. She lived with strong personalities and she felt inadequate. She wasn't as sporty, intelligent, quick-witted, or outgoing as other members of her family. She found it difficult to forge close friendships because she never felt good enough about herself.

At times, she would try to make connections with others, but often felt as though her attempts came out wrong. Sometimes this was because she would try to prove to others why they should like her by being opinionated, or by inappropriately sharing the secrets of others, or by trying to be funny. Other times, she would try to get sympathy by making a big deal out of illnesses or injuries, or using other attention-seeking behaviours.

The result of all this activity was that fewer, not more, people wanted to be her friend. But God came calling, and Laura realised that in Jesus she had found someone who loved her completely. Becoming a Christian was an easy decision – she recognised God's love and also saw in other believers something she didn't have – and she wanted that.

Laura threw herself into her new Christian life with gusto. She joined activities, attended services, and helped out with a youth group. For a while she felt as though she had found Heaven on earth. Yet, underneath she still felt troubled and unworthy. She began to discover she wasn't so good at being a Christian. Others seemed to manage it with ease, but she wasn't one of them.

Laura understood that she ought to show love, joy, peace, patience, kindness, goodness, faithfulness, gentleness, and self-control – the fruit of the Spirit – but she never felt peaceful, struggled to be joyful, and didn't always feel good or kind. She had poor self-control and couldn't break out of old habits of attention-seeking, gossiping, or being opinionated. She concluded that she wasn't a good person and that she made a lousy Christian.

Finally, someone helped her see that God didn't want her to manufacture love, joy, peace, and patience, but that the fruit of the Spirit came from the Spirit. This person helped her understand that her version of the Christian faith was less about her faith in Christ and more about self-effort.

Upon realising this, Laura's life began to change. She gave up trying to be something she was not. She gave up trying to get people to notice her through what she did and said. She gave up pretending to be a Christian. And then, over time, something great happened. The more Laura gave portions of her life over to God, and the more she allowed God to work in her life, the more she learned who she was. And the more she saw what God could do with her if she was willing and available – the more she began to appreciate her good qualities and why God had made her as He did.

Laura learned the truth of 1 Thessalonians 5:24 (emphasis added):

The one who calls you is faithful and *he will do it*.

So those are key areas to bear in mind as you reframe your thinking. This chapter has focused on inward reflection and self-examination. But, as we have seen, God does not want or intend for us to spend the rest of our days as

Re-examining and Reframing

Christians focusing on our inward selves. There comes a time to begin looking outward – this is a vital aspect of transforming mindsets and moving forward. We'll look at that in more detail in the next chapter.

CHAPTER NINE

An Outward Focus

As we have already seen, Jesus gave up His equality with God in order to take on the nature of a servant. He speaks about this in Matthew 20:25-28 when he says,

> You know that the rulers of the Gentiles lord it over them, and that their high officials exercise authority over them. Not so with you. Instead, whoever wants to become great among you must be your servant, and whoever wants to be first must be your slave – just as the Son of Man did not come to be served, but to serve, and to give his life as a ransom for many.

Note that in the last sentence Jesus makes a distinction between serving and sacrifice. He says, 'but to serve, *and* to give his life.' These are two separate things. His service wasn't only to die for us so that we can be saved. He also served as He lived.

In John 13, we read the account of Jesus washing the disciples' feet, a lowly and unpleasant task. He does this in order to demonstrate that even the greatest among us should be willing to undertake the lowest of tasks if need be. In verse 15 he says, 'I have set you an example that you should do as I have done for you.' Here, Jesus isn't saying we should be setting up a foot-washing ministry. Rather, we should emulate His service by ministering to others in whatever way possible – be it a grand task or a small detail.

In a parable about the reckoning that will come at the end of all things, Jesus says to those who were faithful Him:

> For I was hungry and you gave me something to eat, I was thirsty and you gave me something to drink, I was a stranger and you invited me in, I needed clothes and you clothed me, I was sick and you looked after me, I was in prison and you came to visit me. (Matthew 25:35-36)

When the faithful ask in verses 37 to 39,

> Lord, when did we see you hungry and feed you, or thirsty and give you something to drink? When did we see you a stranger and invite you in, or needing clothes and clothe you? When did we see you sick or in prison and go to visit you?

Jesus replies,

> I tell you the truth, whatever you did for one of the least of these brothers of mine, you did for me.

Galatians 5:13-14 tells us,

> You, my brothers, were called to be free. But do not use your freedom to indulge the sinful nature; rather,

serve one another in love. The entire law is summed up in a single command: Love your neighbour as yourself.

In 1 Peter 4:10 we read:

> Each one should use whatever gift he has received to serve others, faithfully administering God's grace in its various forms.

Doesn't that sound wonderful: administering God's grace in its various forms?

And that's the thing about service – there are many ways you can serve. They don't all have to be grand or obvious. In fact, Jesus says in Matthew 6:3-4,

> But when you give to the needy, do not let your left hand know what your right hand is doing, so that your giving may be in secret. Then your Father, who sees what is done in secret, will reward you.

BELINDA'S STORY

Belinda, a faithful Christian, faces a huge barrier to serving God: she is very unwell. Her illness leaves her so tired that even simple tasks like getting up and getting dressed sap her energy to the point where she sometimes needs to sleep afterwards. At times, she feels useless, and that life is passing her by.

A friend of Belinda's runs a ministry supporting a number of schools in developing nations. This friend takes teams of teachers from New Zealand to those nations to help train local teachers in poor and remote schools. They also take with them educational resources.

Belinda can't go on these trips. She can't even support them financially because her illness means she can't work. However, she can write. When her friend was trying to collect books to set up a library in one of these schools, Belinda wrote letters to local publishers of children's books. One of the letters resulted in a donation of a thousand books.

Belinda is able to be an encourager and supporter of others through social media sites like Facebook. While not everyone finds such platforms useful, Belinda now has friends around the world with whom she stays in regular contact. It gives her great satisfaction to be able to help others, pray for them, and provide a distant, but genuine, shoulder to cry on.

We can't all be great speakers or teachers. We can't all donate money or run a ministry like Belinda's friend. Some of us find it difficult to even get out of bed. But, just like Belinda, there will be something we can do. With modern technology, we don't necessarily need to go to the world – the world can come to us.

God has made you to be you. God has given you His salvation in order that you can serve. And, as to what God

An Outward Focus

is trying to accomplish, never forget: it's not your business, and *He will do it*. How can you serve God today?

SERVICE AND HOPE
There are definite benefits to serving others. Here are just a few:

SERVICE BRINGS PERSPECTIVE
Somewhere on the planet there must be someone to whom the phrase, 'It could be worse' does not apply. Chances are, this is not you. Serving others gives you an exciting opportunity to gain perspective. You may feel as though your life is one long drudge of suffering, but by helping others you might discover this isn't as true as you thought. Perspective is vital if you are going to be grateful and find hope.

SERVICE LOOKS FORWARD
As we have already seen, hope looks toward a future event. Lack of hope can be caused as a result of frequently looking back. Service, on the other hand, requires you to make plans, and such plans cause you to look forward. Service also requires you to work in the present – and, as we know, living in the present helps your focus and your wellbeing.

SERVICE CONNECTS TO COMMUNITY
Service often happens shoulder to shoulder with others, and is done for the sake of others. Such endeavours create a sense of community. Many people who lack hope feel isolated and lonely. Connecting to a community provides a great antidote. Getting involved could require you to take risks, but the rewards are more than worthwhile. You can

make new friends, enjoy interesting activities, find ways to help others, and in turn, receive help if and when needed.

Even in Belinda's case, where leaving her house is a challenge, taking part in something bigger than herself and being involved in someone else's ministry is enough to make her feel more connected. Social media enables Belinda to link with others to establish new friendships or build stronger ones with existing and new friends who share a common cause of serving God.

SERVICE HELPS US GROW

In serving others, we are stretched and we grow. This growth may take different forms, but all growth is good. The more we grow, the more we are able to help others and the better we will feel about ourselves. Growth options include mental or intellectual enhancement in learning how others live and adopting problem-solving strategies to help the poor or oppressed learn to deal with their issues. In serving others, we will likely grow spiritually by opening our hearts to people in need. We might also become more aware of certain judgmental attitudes or biases that we have been unknowingly harbouring.

SERVICE HELPS OTHERS GROW

When we serve others, we do so in order that their lives will be enriched. Who knows the result of those books that ended up in Africa? Did one child learn something vital that will benefit the remainder of his or her life? Did even one child feel inspired to take up a particular profession or to develop a new skill that will prove advantageous to many? Sometimes the outcome will be unknown. But, as we saw earlier, we don't need to know what is achieved from what we do. We simply need to do whatever God calls us to do, and let Him work according to His purposes.

SERVICE GIVES HOPE

Since you have chosen to read this book, it's likely that you are aware of and understand the importance of hope – and that you also know what it's like to be short on hope.

You aren't the only one. The world is full of people who need hope. In serving others, you bring hope to them – and you know yourself that receiving hope is a precious gift. Can you be the one to offer hope to someone else? Because, in doing so, you may find that your own life is not as short on hope as it had been. Hope is one of those special gifts that, once shared, increases to bless both giver and receiver.

SERVICE REDEEMS OUR SUFFERING

What you have experienced can be used by God to encourage and help others who are going through a similar situation. There is a kind of wisdom and understanding that comes from dealing with difficult situations that can cause you to be more compassionate and understanding toward others facing difficult challenges. You can use your life experiences to reach out to others in Christ-like love. This is how God works – He uses things that initially seem to be hopeless in order to bring hope and life. You see this pattern throughout the Bible – it's called 'redemption'. And you can be part of His plan in that way.

SERVICE BRINGS BLESSING

In John 12:26, Jesus said,

Hope Rising

> Whoever serves me must follow me; and where I am, my servant will also be. My Father will honour the one who serves me.

Think about that verse. Doesn't being with Jesus and being honoured by the Father sound amazing? It does to me. But, in order to receive this blessing, we must serve God and others by reflecting His love and compassion to those who need it.

Let's end with a thought from Robert Louis Stevenson:

> Judge each day not by the harvest you reap, but by the seeds you plant.

Plant a seed today, and, with God's enabling, who knows what it might grow into?

Questions for Reflection

In what ways do you feel called to serve others here on earth?
_____
_____
_____

What forms of service have you been involved with in the past, and how did they work out?
_____
_____
_____

How have you been blessed through acts of service given to others?
_____
_____
_____

In turn, have you received gifts of service from people that have blessed you in various ways?
_____
_____
_____

Hope Rising

How have your acts of service impacted your Christian hope?
_____
_____
_____

CHAPTER TEN

NOW AND NEXT

As we near the end of this little book, and as you step forward on your journey of hope, I would like to share a few more bits and pieces that I've learnt along the way. These things will help you live in the present and move forward into the future.

BE ACTIVE, NOT PASSIVE

It is tempting in times of trial, when hope seems thin, to become passive. In essence, we freeze under the weight of our burdens. And, if we have learned unhealthy habits through past bad experiences, we may even adopt a victim mentality. We become so sorry for ourselves that we stop trying to understand the circumstances that may be the cause. We become spectators to our misery instead of taking a proactive approach to dealing with the underlying issues.

God doesn't want us to be victims. A proper understanding of the role that suffering can play in our lives (as discussed earlier) is helpful in looking at trials from a healthier perspective. Don't forget the words of Jesus:

> Come to me, all you who are weary and burdened, and I will give you rest. Take my yoke upon you and

> learn from me, for I am gentle and humble in heart, and you will find rest for your souls. For my yoke is easy and my burden is light. (Matthew 11:28-30)

We also need to ask ourselves whether, in feeling sorry for ourselves, we are in fact wanting others to feel sorry for us as well. At its worst, this can be a form of attention-seeking. This may not accurately describe your situation – but it's worth asking yourself honestly if self-pity has taken you to an unhealthy place.

If you are in a difficult situation, try to be productive in escaping it. And, even if you are in a situation (such as ill health, or caring for a relative with needs, or money problems) where getting out is not an option, you still need to make sure you are active about finding support, and moving in a positive direction by doing little things to refresh yourself or that bring you joy.

Make a choice not to be passive. Take action – even baby steps – every day.

START SMALL

Taking action every day is not always about grand or bold moves. A worthwhile action could be as little as making time to talk with a trusted friend, going for a bike ride, or reading Scripture. Relax by the window to enjoy a view of nature's beauty. Sip a cup of refreshing tea or lemonade. Take a walk, hike, or run alone to clear your thoughts, or with a friend to socialise. Listen to uplifting music. Simply smile! Research shows that smiling – even when alone – can actually lift your spirits, and so can singing, alone or with others. With so many fun, interesting, or enjoyable things to do, you can almost certainly help yourself to feel better.

Whatever you do, be deliberate. Start planning positive steps and activities for the future. Be ready to tackle hopelessness when it descends on your spirit. Intentional living will help you be more present. Setting specific small goals will help you look forward and be more hopeful.

Once you take such action – however small – don't forget to express gratitude for the opportunity. In fact, give God a large helping of gratitude while you are at it.

Keep a positive focus

When times are difficult, it is easy to fall into the trap of adopting a negative attitude. Let me give you an example. New parents often find themselves overwhelmed with the responsibility of caring for a newborn, especially if it is their first baby. Infants are exhausting, and looking after them is relentless. Housework and other duties pile up and get neglected as a result of the all-consuming task of tending to a baby's needs. You might feel as though the rest of your life has gone by the wayside because of your single-minded devotion to caring for your helpless infant.

In such times, it can be tempting to look at all you haven't done and feel bad. You may think you aren't coping or that you should be able to manage better. You might feel guilty because you've let things you normally manage drop by the wayside. But take a deep breath, pause for a moment, and see the positives. If, at the end of the day, your baby is well-fed and well-cared for, what does the rest matter? Is there any greater task on this planet than protecting, loving, and caring for a tiny child? Is any other job more crucial than that? Everything else can wait. Your baby will grow up soon enough.

No matter the challenges of life, focus on what you have achieved, not on what you haven't. Be kind to yourself. Know that God is gracious and loving. Apply yourself to making good, deliberate, and realistic choices each day – ones that are geared positively rather than negatively. Your outlook can make a massive difference.

ENJOY CREATION

Modern life tends to drive us away from creation. We spend time indoors or in cars on the road. We hurry from place to place. We live in a world increasingly dominated by technology – machinery that sometimes attracts and holds our attention for unhealthy periods of time.

Yet, the great outdoors is just that – great. The beauty of creation can provide a balm to our souls, if only we let it. Not only that, exercise and fresh air have proven benefits for our wellbeing – both mentally and physically.

Ask yourself this: When did you last take a close look at a lilac or a rose, or study the intricacies of a spider's web? When did you last walk barefoot on the grass or on a beach? When did you last take a walk away from an urban environment? When did you last go out exploring, and embrace a sense of adventure and play?

Take time to get back to nature. You will find God – and hope.

GET SOUND ADVICE

If you're feeling stuck in your circumstances, or your situation is complex, you may need help and support from a professional. Take active steps to find such help. In the back of this book, there is a short directory of programs and agencies you can turn to in New Zealand. Finding a good counsellor is often a life-changing step – someone to walk alongside you, provide a listening ear, and offer trained advice. Pray that God leads you to the best person to understand your needs. No man (or woman) is an island, and we are not meant to live alone. We are relational beings, and we aren't supposed to fight our way through life independent of others who want to share our burdens and lift our spirits.

Don't look at getting help as a sign of weakness or let pride stand in the way of improving your life. Consider this help as the opportunity to learn new skills. And, in the learning and implementing of new abilities, great change may come to pass.

HAVE COURAGE

The author William Faulkner said,

> You cannot swim for new horizons until you have courage to lose sight of the shore.

This is an interesting idea but with one important qualification: as Christians, we are fortunate to have God as our guide. If He calls us to aim for new horizons, He will come alongside us. However, we need to be prepared to take that first all-important step.

The opposite of courage is fear. If your life is dominated by fear, look again at your mindset, at your understanding of

Hope Rising

God, and at your relationship with Him. What is holding you back? What do you feel might stand in the way of success?

Remember, having courage is making a choice to trust God – who is faithful and mighty. We can count on His help, every step of the way.

BE ACCOUNTABLE

Now, you may not see yourself as needing help in the sense of seeking professional advice. In fact, you may not see yourself as needing advice at all. That's fine. Not all of us need that sort of outside intervention.

However, most of us can do with some encouragement. That's where an accountability partner can be useful. An accountability partner is a trusted person who you could talk to about any issues you're facing in life. This person could periodically check in with you, encourage you to keep journaling, and see how you're doing as you work on being transformed by the renewing of your mind. That person might wish to disclose his or her struggles to you. The accountability could be mutual between you.

Such a person can be a great ally in the process of changing your thinking, bringing a broader perspective to your situation and outlook. A relationship like that will help you feel less isolated and more connected to the world around you.

TAKE RESPONSIBILITY

Hopefully by now you have taken an honest look at your life – at how you think, at what you do (or don't do), at the choices you make – and have realised the ways in which you may have been undermining your sense of hope. If you have observed areas that need attention, take responsibility for making improvements. Don't let pride get in the way of making new and better choices.

KEEP LEARNING

Many of us have a tendency to get to a certain point in our lives and feel as though we can't be bothered learning new things. However, the world is full of interesting ideas, and there is always more we can learn. By staying interested and learning new things, even in a small way, you can help yourself to become more aware and more hopeful in the present.

And don't stop learning about God. As we saw earlier in Romans 11:33:

> Oh, the depth of the riches of the wisdom and knowledge of God!

There are endless things we can learn about our Lord.

DON'T JUST CONSUME, CREATE

In our crazy, time-poor world it can be tempting to give up creating things and instead consume the creations of others. Online platforms offer endless shows to watch. We carry books on our phones. We spend hours looking at other people's lives on social media. Consume, consume, consume.

Yet, we are creative beings, and we can gain great satisfaction in creating something new. This doesn't have to be art, music, prose, or poetry. Not everyone's interests are the same. You could choose to create a garden or decorate a cake or make something with your hands. It doesn't have to be a big thing – and it doesn't have to be perfect. The deliberate creation of something new requires your attention and helps you look forward to the future. The act of creation can lift our spirits and enable us to see the future with hope.

GIVE HOPE TO OTHERS
Former US president Barack Obama said:

> The best way to not feel hopeless is to get up and do something. Don't wait for good things to happen to you. If you go out and make some good things happen, you will fill the world with hope, and you will fill yourself with hope.

This is so true.

Our role as servants of God is to reach out to others, to serve others. Consider what you could do to serve someone else, and, in the process, find hope for yourself.

Let's now look to set some goals for your new 'now' and 'next' point of view.

QUESTIONS FOR REFLECTION

What practical steps are you going to take to deal with the external things (e.g. events, insults, rejections, or grief) that have happened to you?

_____

_____

_____

What do you need to do to improve your internal state in terms of your sense of hope?

_____

_____

_____

What are the specific actions (in keeping with such things as enjoying creation, getting sound advice, learning, creating, and giving hope to others) that you could take to more fully embrace your life?

_____

_____

_____

_____

What choices have you made that you need to take responsibility for?

_____
_____
_____
_____

What choices can you make that will get your life heading in a more positive or hopeful direction?

_____
_____
_____
_____

How are you going to connect with our God of hope and maintain this connection?

_____
_____
_____
_____

Final Thoughts

As we come to the end of this book, I want to take this opportunity to wish you well. Life is an adventure, and God has good things in store for you as He uses what you've been through to mature you into a more loving and hopeful person. Use this book as an ongoing resource, especially if you strike fresh times of trouble that test your hope. After all, life is a journey; its circumstances ever changing.

Staying connected to God as the source of goodness in life is our greatest hope, as we keep a clear mindset about our place as His servants and hold our expectations lightly. Even in the darkest times and even when He feels far away, know that God loves you. Through good actions and choices, partner with Him in the transformation of your outlook on life. Practise gratitude and look for opportunities to be there for others.

Always remember the words of Paul in Romans 12:1-2:

> Therefore, I urge you, brothers, in view of God's mercy, to offer your bodies as living sacrifices, holy and pleasing to God – this is your spiritual act of worship. Do not conform any longer to the pattern of this world but be transformed by the renewing of your

mind. Then you will be able to test and approve what God's will is – his good, pleasing and perfect will.

I pray that as you walk life's path, you will discover more and more the faithfulness of God, and that His love, kindness, peace and HOPE will fill your heart.

Help Directory

If you feel uncertain or overwhelmed, or you just need to talk, reach out to people who can help. If you live in New Zealand, here are two useful online directories:

- Find a Christian counsellor: www.nzcca.org.nz/member-directory/
- Community helplines: www.mentalhealth.org.nz/get-help/in-crisis/helplines/

Acknowledgements

To my family and friends, thank you for your continuous love and magnanimous support over the years. In particular I would like to mention the following people (please forgive any inadvertent omissions): Michaella Kim; Christopher Parvathy and Chantal Asairigadu; Dr Joseph and Delores D'Allende; Pastor Sunil and Dr Sunitha, Jessica and Megan Sooknundan; Will, Ruby and Josh Wilson; Andrew Killick (Castle Publishing); Anna and Kevin Van Noorwyk; Dean and Daisy Shunmugam; Congregation of Calvary Ministries, Chatsworth, Durban; Vinny and Kassie Sooknundan; Pastor Ramesh and Halley Sheodin; Ricky Sheodin and family; Dr Kai Yin Chau and family; Evangelist Justus Ondieki (Kenya); Tony and Sera Schwalger; Abraham, Sunitha and family Vasanthraj; Melanie and Premilla Naidoo; Kamla and Moses Luke; Mohan and Rosalind Ori; Pastor Johnny and family; Teresa Iakop and family; Moi Martin and family.

About the Author

Born in South Africa, Jacob Isaac was the co-founder and senior pastor of Calvary Ministries in Durban. He now lives in New Zealand and has held various leadership positions within the health sector and in manufacturing. As well as acting as a life coach and motivational speaker, he serves on the leadership board of Calvary Apostolic International Ministries, with a focus on prophecy teaching. This is his first book.

ABOUT THE AUTHOR

Born in South Africa, Jacob Isaak was the co-founder and senior pastor of Calvary Ministries in Durban. He now lives in New Zealand and has held various leadership positions within the Health sector and in mentoring/tutoring. As well as being an elite coach and motivational speaker, he also focuses on his friendship brand of Calvary Apostolic Ministries Ministries, with a focus on prophecy teaching. This is his first book.